THE ONEONTA
FAIR

AIR SHIP AT CENTRAL N. Y. FAIR, ONEONTA, N. Y., SEPT. 1906.

Jim Loudon

Square Circle Press
Voorheesville, New York

The Oneonta Fair
by Jim Loudon

Published by
Square Circle Press LLC
137 Ketcham Road
Voorheesville, NY 12186
www.squarecirclepress.com

First American paperback edition, 2013.
Printed and bound in the United States of America on acid-free, durable paper.
ISBN 13: 978-0-9856926-4-3
ISBN 10: 0-9856926-4-2
Library of Congress Control Number: 2013939162

Publisher's Acknowledgments
Cover ©2013 by Square Circle Press; design by Richard Vang.

Photo credits: Unless otherwise noted, all images are from the Greater Oneonta Historical Society Collection (Oneonta, New York). "NYSHA" refers to the New York State Historical Association (Cooperstown, New York).

The acknowledgments of the Author appear elsewhere in this book.

Official Program

ACKNOWLEDGMENTS

The primary sources for this book were the *Oneonta Herald* (1872-1927), the *Oneonta Star* (1890-1927), and *In Old Oneonta, Volume 1*, by Edwin R. Moore (The Village Printer, Laurens, New York, 1963). I am deeply indebted to Bob Brzozowski and the Greater Oneonta History Society for allowing me to include images from their extensive collection; the staff at Huntington Library in Oneonta, the New York State Historical Association Library in Cooperstown, the Oneonta Daily Star, and the Milne Library at the State University of New York at Oneonta for their assistance with the necessary research to produce this book; Marc Bresee for the use of his postcard collection; and my fiancé Jo Tufano for putting in many long hours typing and proofreading.

The Oneonta

FAIR

INTRODUCTION

By 1872 Oneonta had become a thriving community of just under 2,000 souls, a direct result of the Albany and Susquehanna Railroad's arrival in 1865, and the village's subsequent designation as the company's primary shop facility between Binghamton and Albany. This prosperous environment provided the impetus for a group of Oneonta businessmen to organize the Oneonta Union Agricultural Society in late summer 1872, electing Allen Scrambling as President. The intent of the organization was to develop an agricultural fair, but there was no progress toward that goal until the following year.

After fire consumed his bank and hop exchange in Milford during the latter part of December 1872, Oneonta's growing prosperity convinced David Wilber to relocate his business interests to Oneonta the following year, setting up shop in the Walter Brown Hardware Store at the corner of Main and Dietz Streets. From the time they arrived in Oneonta, David and his sons, George I. and David F., strove to advance the interests of their adopted home. His banking business expanded rapidly, and in 1876 he relocated to larger quarters in the Central Hotel building.

In 1873 David and his landlord (and close friend) Walter Brown embarked on an endeavor that would benefit the village of Oneonta for decades to come. In that year the two businessmen reorganized the Oneonta Union Agricultural Society, determined to establish a yearly exhibition and fair. A large section of the Couse farm in East End was purchased and crews were set to work clearing and grading the site.

There was great anticipation prior to the first Fair to be held in October of 1873, which proved to be a genuine success for the promoters. Over the following years the Fair became a major boon for the local economy, filling the village with thousands of visitors from across the state for one week, which generated significant revenue for the railroads and trolley line. The Fair's promoters made every effort to provide new attractions that would maximize attendance; there were marriages at the Roof Garden, gymnasts, balloon ascensions, and later, a "Birdman," who brought the first airplane to Central New York. Trotting races were a big draw from the time the Fairgrounds opened, and the Floral Parade was the most anticipated event of the year.

In 1873 Fair Street was opened to provide easy access from Otsego Street, and in 1888 the Oneonta Street Railway opened a branch from Main Street to the Fairgrounds.

The Fair meant two afternoons out of school for local children, and the trolley line ran open cars up Tilton Avenue and over Fair Street to the festivities. Downtown Oneonta was packed with pitchmen on every corner and, for many years, Charles K. Champlin and his repertory company performed at the Oneonta Theater during Fair Week, offering plays borrowed from Broadway.

The Floral Parade was always a grand display, offering local businesses an opportunity to advertise through their lavish floats. Prizes were awarded for the most impressive displays, and prize winners paraded again the following day. The Fair also provided an opportunity for politicians to greet large numbers of people, and notables included Teddy Roosevelt in 1899 and his cousin Franklin Delano Roosevelt in 1915.

Attendance for the Fair peaked at 30,000 on September 21, 1910, but with the coming of the automobile, fewer visitors stayed in the village and Fair receipts began to dwindle. George I. Wilber, the driving force behind the Fair, died in 1922 and there was no one left to champion the cause. In 1923 D.F. Keyes purchased the outstanding shares of the organization, and in 1927 he commenced selling off building lots on the old Fairgrounds. The development was originally called Belmont Park, and over 100 homes were built on the grounds where thousands of fairgoers once congregated for the most exciting week of the year.

Little remains of the Oneonta Fairgrounds today; Belmont Circle is the original race track, and visages of the concrete Grandstand piers and retaining wall are still visible behind the homes on North Belmont Circle. Looking at what little remains, it might be hard to imagine that Oneonta once hosted the second largest fair in New York State.

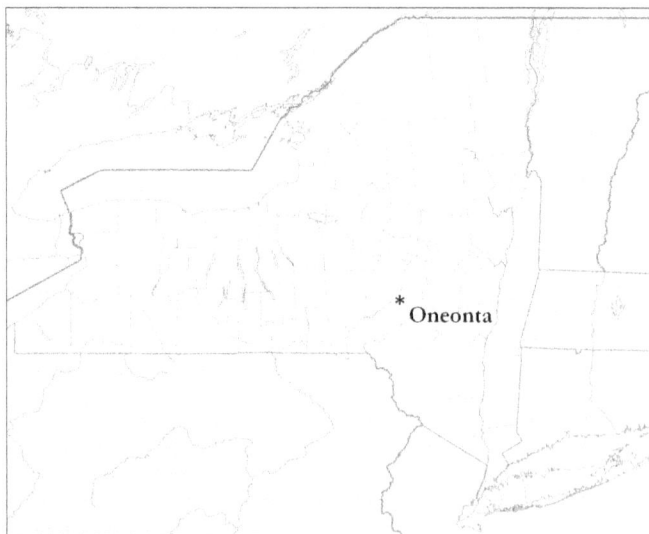

Oneonta's location in Central New York State, nestled along the banks of the Susquehanna River in Otsego County.

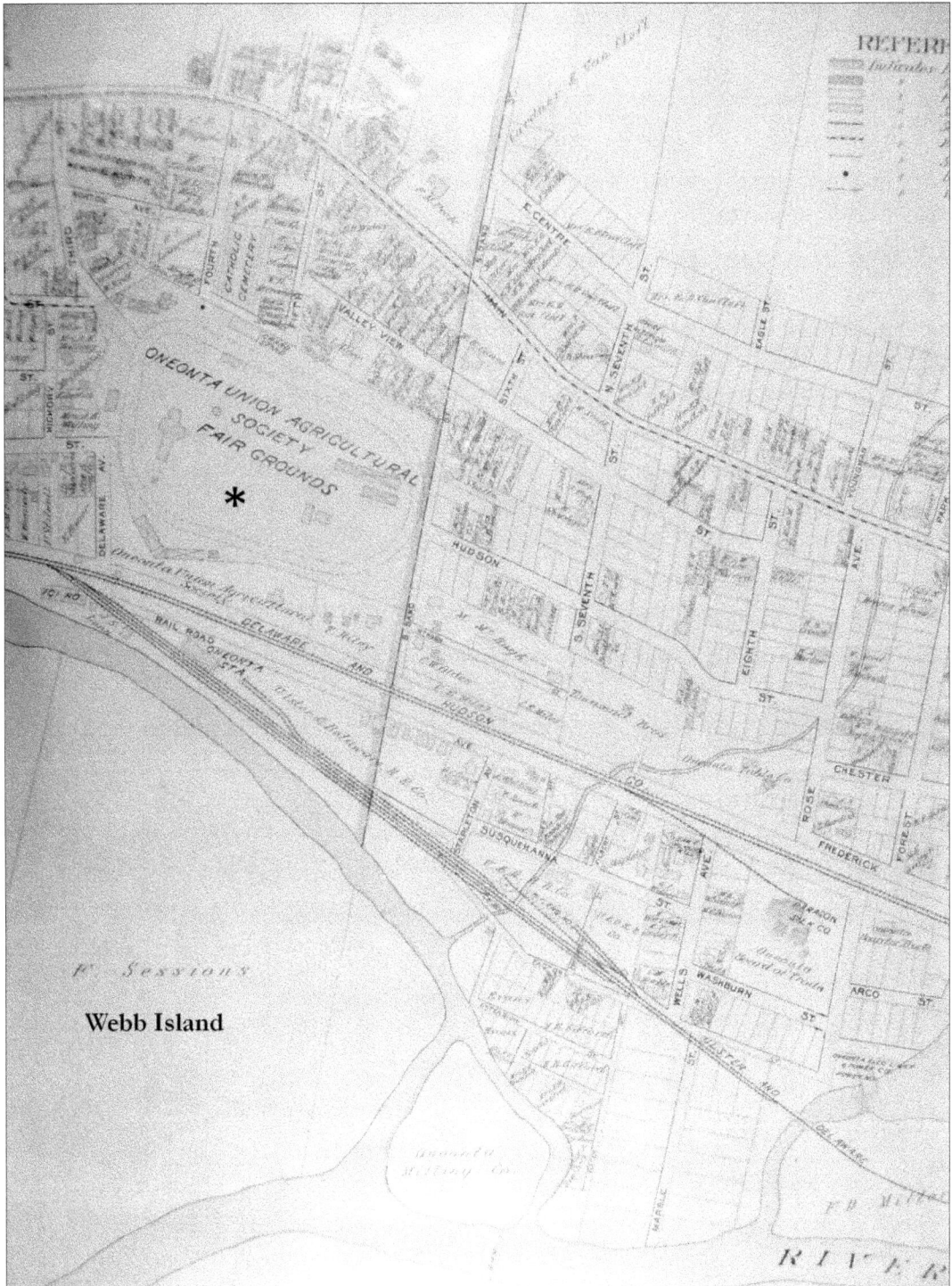

Oneonta, with the sites of the original fair (*) and the 1949 fair on Webb Island.

A Fair is Born

1873 was a hectic year for the bustling village of Oneonta; a new brick building was erected by E.D. Saunders and William McCrum at the corner of Main and Broad Streets (now gone); several new streets were laid out, including Clinton, Ernst (Irving Place), Luther, Burnside and Green (Columbia). A third story was added to the Eagle Hotel, and the Albany and Susquehanna filled the swamp adjacent to the depot in anticipation of marketing commercial properties. The talk of the business community centered around the relocation of David Wilber's bank to the Brown Hardware building on Main Street, and by mid-January he had commenced placing ads for his new banking business on the front page of the *Oneonta Herald*. Mr. Wilber had been recently elected to the U.S. House of Representatives, and it was anticipated that his business acumen and political connections would greatly benefit the growing community.

Mr. Wilber did not disappoint his new neighbors, as the year he moved to Oneonta was also the year he reorganized the Oneonta Agricultural Society along with Walter Brown, the purpose of which was to develop an annual fair and exhibition. One of the

Left: David Wilber's first bank was located at the corner of East and North Main Streets in Milford. Right: David Wilber's second bank was opened in 1873 on the first floor of the Brown Hardware Store at the corner of Main and Dietz Streets in Oneonta.

initial stockholder meetings for the new venture was held in mid-April at The Susque-hanna House on Main Street, with Vice-President E.C. Bundy presiding. A resolution was adopted authorizing J.R.L. Walling to make a final survey for the race track, and committees were appointed to let the grading and fencing work out to the lowest re-sponsible bidder, and to purchase additional land from Mr. Walling. The committee was comprised of Jay McDonald, S.M. Ballard, and W.W. Snow. The printing of additional stock subscriptions and 500 lifetime tickets were also approved. Of the $6,000 capital stock, all but $1,800 had been subscribed and 70% of that had been paid in. The stock-holders were confident in their investment and the future of the Oneonta Fair seemed assured.

At this point the promoters decided it was prudent to recover some of their invest-ment prior the opening of the Fair, so it was announced that there would be horse races on the new race track on the Fourth of July. By the middle of May crews were at work grading and fencing the grounds; the grading contract had been awarded to A.V. Kibble, and the fencing to Harrison White. An acre of land adjoining the grounds was purchased from Mr. Walling for $200, and for an additional $250, he opened a street through the property (Fair Street), fenced it and deeded the right-of-way.

Throughout May and June, Jay McDonald worked tirelessly overseeing the work of preparing the grounds and track in preparation for the July 4 opening race. To attract a high caliber of entrants, the promoters advertised a generous purse of $525, to be di-vided as follows: First purse, $175; $100 to first place; $50 to second; $25 to third. The sweepstakes would pay $200 to first place, $100 to second, and $50 to third. The races were well-attended, with first place winners bearing names like "Topsey," "Shoo-fly," and "Crazy." In following years the Fourth of July races would become a regular event, advertised as the races at Oneonta Park, to distinguish itself from the Fair races.

Once the track had been re-groomed from the trotters, the Fair Managers had to settle on a date for the first fair to take place, and the dates selected were October 1-3. There was some concern that the timing was a problem, as the opening was taking place several weeks after the end of fair season. However, the promoters believed it was more important to have the grounds in pristine condition before admitting the public. An *Oneonta Herald* editorial in May 1873 encouraged the Managers to make every effort to include not only livestock and animal displays, but also local manufactured items and ladies' specialties, so that visitors would not remember the fair as simply an "agricultural horse trot."

The first Oneonta Fair opened to beautiful weather on Thursday, October 1, and the sunshine continued into Friday, and on that day locals witnessed the largest gather-ing of people in the village's history. The opening was somewhat marred by the pres-ence of local scammers, who cheated many visitors out of their quarters on the wheel and dice games, leaving many with a poor first impression of the event. The overall re-sponse was positive, however, as the promoters had worked diligently to provide a wide variety of attractions. There was "Educated Ben," the amazing pig who had learned how to count along with trained horses, and the amazing two-headed calf. Punch and Judy was re-enacted at the open air theater.

One of the more unique attractions was a crank-operated "circular swing," which consisted of wooden seats and carved horses similar to a carousel, and which delighted fair-goers of all ages. Miss Hill of the village created a highly-detailed diorama of a cot-tage situated in a park-like setting, with fountains, trees, and a lake. On Thursday after-noon a ball game was played on the green, featuring two teams from Laurens, the "Fearless" and the "Unprofessional." For those not attracted to baseball, a horse race was run at the same time, offering a $15 purse to the winners. Two horses were entered, Charles Halock's "Brown George" of Schenevus, and Al Parson's black mare from Af-ton. "Brown George" won the first heat and the mare won the second and third.

On Friday afternoon a large crowd gathered in the rear of the large tent to hear an address given by Professor Potter of Cornell University on the importance of farming and how recent scientific discoveries had benefited the farmer, while highlighting the need for farmers to educate themselves in order to benefit from the latest advances.

The promoters offered a diverse roster of awards, with a total of 367 prizes in 29 categories, which included the traditional specialties such as livestock, sheep and fowl, in addition to hops, artwork, sports, and domestic manufactures. As the first Oneonta Fair drew to a close, the board members felt confident that their initial endeavor had been an overwhelming success, and they anticipated growing and improving the event in the following years.

Walter Brown

David Wilber

THROUGH THE YEARS

The second Oneonta Fair commenced on September 22, 1874, and continued for two more days. For the second year of the event, the Board of Managers decided to keep the horse racing purse as a minimal amount of the total prize monies, $160 out of $2,250. There was a good deal of new construction at the Fairgrounds during the spring and summer of 1874; business partners A.D. Shumway of Cooperstown and A.P. Harber of Morris erected a shed that would serve as a tavern for the Fair, and a substantial structure was built to provide an exhibition hall which would be known as Floral Hall. The building was one story with a pitched roof, approximately 25' x 80', with two adjacent east and west wings (25' x 25'), and a center cupola. A Judge's Stand was erected next to the track.

A week of wet weather preceded the opening on Wednesday, but the crowds were blessed with a sunny first day of the Fair, and Main Street witnessed a parade of carriages headed toward East End such as the village had never seen before. The Fair always provided a showcase for the latest advances in agriculture, and among the attractions in 1874 were the new Phelps hand-digging potato fork, and an improved butter churn displayed by H.H. Wheeler of Otsego County. Other exhibits included wagons, parlor stoves, and a music wagon, provided by the Kneeland Brothers, that entertained fairgoers throughout all three days.

The Fair prospered over the following years, continually offering new attractions. In 1876, the first two days saw steady rain, but receipts still set a record of nearly $1,500 for the three-day event. Unfortunately, as Fair attendance continued to increase, so did public drunkenness; prior to the 1877 event the General Superintendent issued a prohibition on the sale of liquor, and officials were instructed to escort visitors away from the grounds who had imbibed too much lager. Apparently these actions were effective, as the *Oneonta Herald* reported that the Fairgrounds were much more peaceful than in previous years. In the following fairs beer was also restricted, but it was reintroduced in 1881, due to popular demand.

The 1882 Fair was a landmark event for the Board of Directors, setting a record of $2,400 in receipts, which allowed the outstanding debt to be retired, while still retaining a surplus for investment in further improvements, which would include a cattle barn and new fencing. When the Fair opened for its tenth anniversary in 1883, several improvements greeted the fairgoers, including a secretary's office and a livestock barn.

The main attraction at the 1884 Fair was one the Managers had not planned on; it seems that a couple of young "cowboys," who had had a few too many beers, showed up on the grounds dressed in pants and long johns, but no shirts or coats, and both had revolvers protruding from their belts. After waving their pistols at terrified visitors, they moved on to the Central Hotel, where the local police were summoned due to their threatening behavior. Officer Seeger arrested the two, and while en route to the jail, one of the boys removed his revolver to hand it to his brother, which the officer saw as a threat and responded with several blows from a billy club. The boys went to court the following Tuesday and explained to Judge Scott that they were on the way back to their home in Windsor and, after listening to several witnesses, the Judge apparently felt that officer Seeger had used excessive force and dismissed the charges, allowing the two cowboys to retrieve their pistols and paddle a canoe back to their home.

Weddings at the Fair were a popular annual event, but did not always go according to plan. In 1886, a wedding was scheduled between George Lee and Anna Sykes of Binghamton. A few days before the event, Mr. Lee made it known to the Fair Managers that not only was he not going to get married on the Fairgrounds, but he "was not going to marry that Sykes girl anyway!" This left the Managers in a scramble to find a replacement couple.

Oneonta was alive with excitement in the summer of 1888, as word of a new sensation at the fair traveled thru the community: for the first time there was to be a balloon ascension! Professor Price thrilled fairgoers as his brightly-colored balloon gracefully ascended from the Fairgrounds, but the initial excitement was transcended by his accomplice Lady Viola, who fearlessly leaped from the basket at 300 feet and, after cushioning her descent with the aid of a parachute, she landed safely on the grounds to the delight of the audience. The balloon ascent continued to be a major attraction in succeeding fairs.

By the 1890's the Oneonta event had acquired the title "Central New York Fair," and the Floral Parade

Balloon ascension at the Oneonta Fair (date unknown).

had evolved into one of the most popular attractions. This event allowed local merchants the opportunity to construct elaborate floats, decorated with ornate flower arrangements advertising their business to all in attendance. The Delaware and Hudson entry was always one of the most elaborate floats, prepared at the company greenhouse, near the shops. The parade of floats would be drawn along Main and Otsego Streets, and then over the race track. Many times the parade would be run for a second day to maximize exposure for the local businesses who depended heavily on the additional income generated by the yearly event. The stores would run special ads during Fair Week, and the *Oneonta Star* and *Herald* would furnish supplements highlighting the newest attractions.

The 1895 Fair featured hose company drills and a fireworks display, but the real excitement centered around the balloon ascension. Due to mechanical problems the balloon did not fill properly, but not wanting to disappoint the crowd, the balloonist proceeded with the ascent. Unfortunately, the balloon was unable to gain altitude and became tangled in the telegraph lines; luckily there were no injuries as a result of the mishap. In 1897 the Managers decided to reinvest a share of the profits into improving the grounds. The 1893 Grandstand was enlarged, an annex was added to Floral Hall, and a raised platform for performers was attached to the Judge's Stand. The platform would be known as the "Roof Garden."

The Floral Parade of 1898 bore special significance, as it honored the Country's recent victories in the Spanish-American War. The Grand Army of the Republic float featured an elaborate floral reproduction of one of the eight-inch guns that was decisive in the Battle of Santiago, and riding alongside the replica was Ambrose Hamm, a survivor of the "Maine" explosion. The patriotic theme was continued with the Union School float, which carried a giant American flag made of over 13,000 flowers. The Delaware and Hudson float was thought by many to be the most unique entry, consisting of a floral replica of the "Stourbridge Lion," the first locomotive to be run in America. The engine incorporated over 30,000 flowers, all harvested at the company's greenhouse. The judges were obviously impressed, as the D&H float won the sweepstakes prize. It appears that pickpockets had become a problem at the Fair, as several thefts totaling over $700 were reported.

In 1899 the Central New York Fair saw a record attendance of over 15,000 on Wednesday, when the Floral Parade was combined with a visit from Governor Theodore Roosevelt. Trains, trolleys and streets were filled with eager fairgoers headed toward the Fairgrounds. The Floral Parade was grander than ever, with the usual rival floats of the Steamer Hose Company and Wilber Hose Company, and once again Delaware and Hudson captured the sweepstakes prize with a float entitled "The Crowning of Dewey," commemorating the Admiral's victory in the Spanish-American War.

Floral Parade float representing the battleship "Maine."

Float celebrating the naval victories of Dewey in the Spanish-American War.

A popular event for many years was the friendly competition between the Steamer Company and the Wilber Hose Company for first prize in the Floral Parade.

The arrival of Governor Roosevelt was greeted with great fanfare; his special train from Walton was announced by the booming of the D&H shop whistles. The Governor delivered his speech from the Roof Garden in front of the Grandstand, and for about thirty minutes he devoted a speech to the recent Dreyfus Affair, which had occupied France for several months. Mr. Roosevelt lamented that our "sister republic" had allowed itself to be caught up in a wave of antisemitism, and warned that America must remain diligent in judging a man by his personal qualities, not his religious beliefs. After his speech was completed, Governor Roosevelt met with many local dignitaries and toured the grounds, stating that the crowd in attendance was one of the largest he had met throughout the state.

Floral Hall was always a center of activity, and 1899 was no exception. The building incorporated a variety of exhibits in several departments; the Ladies Department offered samples of embroidery and needlework, while the Art Department showcased local talent in painting and photography. Highlights included a a portrait of well-known Oneonta physician Dr. Meigs Case, rendered by his daughter Miss Anna Case, and "artistic images" displayed by local photographer P.R. Young. The Relics Department included displays of clocks, spinning wheels, and flintlock muskets and pistols, in addition to extensive collections of coins and paper money.

The Floral Hall Agricultural Annex showcased fruits and vegetables produced on area farms, and in addition to permanent buildings, numerous merchants erected tents on the grounds to market their wares, including stoves, wagons, and musical instruments. A great deal of attention was attracted by the J.P. Butts display of Crawford Wagons, which were available with pneumatic tires. As always, the cattle barns were busy, housing such breeds as Ayrshires and Belted Dutch, while the sheep pens included Cheviots, Shropshires, and Merinos. The horse races continued to be a vital element of the Fair, with entrants coming from as far away as Cortland and Rochester to participate in purses ranging from $200 to $500.

The Colonel W.W. Snow

For over three decades a cherished sight at the Fair was the Colonel W.W. Snow steam-powered pumper, lovingly decorated by the Oneonta Steamer Company. The steamer was named after Colonel W.W. Snow, the prominent Oneonta merchant who was also Village President and Oneonta's first Congressman. The Colonel was also one of the most ambitious supporters of the Albany and Susquehanna Railroad. The Colonel Snow steamer resided in the fire station on Main Street in Oneonta. A pair of horses was kept in stalls in the basement apparatus room, and the harnesses were balanced on a pulley arrangement in front of the wagon. When an alarm sounded, the stall chains would drop and the horses took their place under the harness. A quick pull and the harness would drop on the horses' backs, and after a few snaps were fastened, the rig was ready to go. The Colonel Snow itself was kept in the rear of the firehouse and was connected by a pipe to a stove in the basement so that there would always be hot water in the boiler, and materials for a fire were kept in the firebox. The steamer horses were kept in the basement and when harnessed they were led up a ramp to the first floor and hitched to the pumper. The pipe was disconnected and the vehicle rolled out the door, and as it cleared the building, a fireman threw a torch into the firebox, which ignited the fire almost immediately. If the fire was any distance away, a full head of steam would be up on arrival.

The Colonel W.W. Snow and crew.

Evolution of the Oneonta Fairgrounds

1884

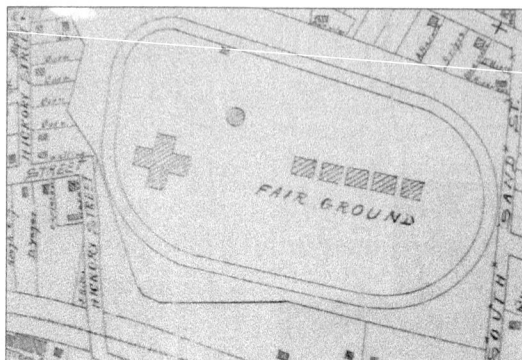
1890

1903

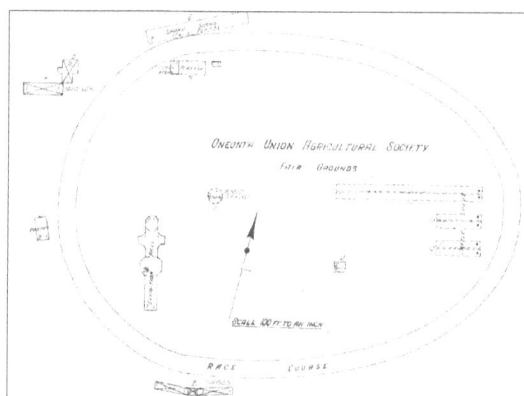
1910

Prior to 1900 three horse barns were added to the Fairgrounds: two were built at the west end of the track near the entrance (above) and measured 25' x 45' and 25' x 60'; another barn, consisting of two angled wings and a two-story center section (below), was built on the south side of the track near the bluff and measured 20' x 110'. The ticket booth was located just to the right of the large barn at Fair Street.

The Roof Garden

The Roof Garden always provided a stage for special attractions at the Fair, hosting magicians, animal acts, weddings, political speeches, acrobats, and even the Golden Globe of Death! It consisted of a raised platform 25 feet deep and 40 feet wide, with a height of 8 feet, and was constructed in 1897 as an extension of the Judge's Stand, which was built in 1874. There were windows on the front and back of the structure, and the inside floor was below ground level in order to provide space for a dining room. For many years the restaurant was operated by the Brown family and was known as Brown's Dining Hall.

Fairground Improvements Prior to 1900

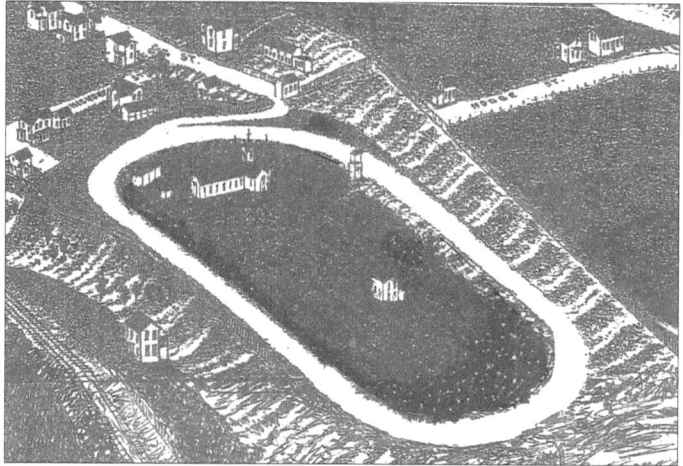

Oneonta Fairground in 1884; Left to right: Cattle Barn (20' x 40'), built in 1883, removed prior to 1890; Tavern Shed (10' x 15'), built in 1874, removed prior to 1890; Exhibition (Floral) Hall, (25' x 80' with two 25' x 25' wings), built in 1874, enlarged in 1897 and 1904, removed in 1927; Judge's Stand, two stories (25' x 25'), built 1873-74, removed in 1927; Secretary's Office, two stories (25' x 35'), built in 1883, removed prior to 1900.

The original Floral Hall was built in 1874 and measured 25' x 80', with two 25' x 25' wings and a center cupola. In 1897 a three-story, 30' x 30' pagoda was added to the north end of the building.

In the late 1880's a two-story, 25-foot diameter Bandstand was erected near the center of the Midway; it was removed in 1927.

The original Grandstand was built in 1893 against the bluff north of the race track. In 1897 it was enlarged to 30' x 120' and bleachers were added between the stand and the track. It was removed in 1910 when the new steel Grandstand was built.

The New Century

As the 20th century dawned, the Central New York Fair was destined to host what many at the time would consider incredible inventions, including the automobile and the airplane. The first Fair of the new century opened to sunny weather on Monday, September 10, 1900. The Fair Managers boasted, "This Fair always performs more than advertised," and most fairgoers would agree that this assertion was in no way presumptuous. As always the cattle barn hosted many prize-winning herds, with several awards going to the Brookside Farm of Milford. A new attraction for the new century was the ostrich races, and the ostrich pens provided a fascination for the young fairgoers.

In spite of windstorms, the last day of the Fair on Wednesday was the busiest of the week. The D&H trains were full on every run, and the Ulster and Delaware ran two extra trains, one from Kingston and one from Fleischmanns. Even with the added capacity, many would-be passengers were left behind between Hobart and Oneonta. The Floral Parade, which had far surpassed previous years, was repeated on the last day. The

The world's only trotting ostrich.

Delaware and Hudson deviated from previous events with a political tone: "Enlightenment versus Barbarism." The horse races were well-attended, with "Brotonane" of Cortland winning the 2:25 heat and "Montana Union" taking first place in the 2:40 race.

For the first time automobiles were seen at the fair, with four machines on the grounds. The autos were all driven form a distance; there were two from Binghamton owned by Roy Whipple and L.R. Clinton, one owned by T.E. Norton of Syracuse, and the fourth owned by Issac Van Etten of Yonkers. The last day of the fair included two balloon ascensions and a race between the four autos, won by Roy Whipple.

The Fair of 1901 was delayed for a week due to the assassination of President McKinley on September 6. Once underway, the newest attraction was a pair of horses, "Hummingbird" and "Nan Wilkes." What made these animals unique was that they were ridden by two dogs! Not only did "Hex" and "Rex" guide the equines around the track, the pairs actually raced each other. As always, the balloon ascension was well-attended, but the "aeronaut" canceled his launch from a giant cannon after discovering that some of his parachute ropes had been cut.

In 1902 a record crowd of 15,000 for the second day of the Fair was present to receive the speech given by Governor O'Dell. This figure was bettered on the following day when 25,000 were on hand to view the Floral Parade. The Delaware and Hudson provided an elaborate, animated float depicting their Oneonta shops in operation, and J.L. Bowdish drove his highly-decorated automobile, the first to appear in the parade. In 1903 the Floral Parade set another record, with a crowd estimated at over 25,000. After 1900 daytime fireworks displays became a popular attraction at the Fair.

In 1904 the Floral Hall underwent a major renovation and expansion. The ambitious reconstruction project involved the addition of two new components: a three-story, 40' x 40' rotunda on the south end of the building, and extending south from the middle rotunda, a 25' x 45' wing with a clerestory roof. The additions gave the Floral

John L. Bowdish's automobile in the Floral Parade, 1902.

Hall a total footprint of 25' x 150', excepting the additional width at the center and north rotundas.

The large rotunda housed an assembly room and the art gallery, displaying drawings, paintings and photography rendered by local artists. The new south wing served as an exhibition hall for Oneonta merchants, including M. Gurney and Sons carpets, furs an cloaks; G.B. Shearer Company pianos and musical instruments; Laurens and Rowe crockery and Oneonta souvenirs, plus hardware and stoves from the firm of Stevens and Baker. There was also a postcard booth maintained by George H. Chandler of the Oneonta Department Store.

The north wing and the small rotunda contained domestic manufactures, ladies handiwork, historic relics, fruits and vegetables and culinary displays. In addition to the merchandise inside the remodeled building, there were numerous dealer tents set up outside, including Arthur M. Butts automobile and carriage sales, and L.B. Murdock's extensive array of International Harvester machinery. Although renamed The Liberal Arts Building, locals still referred to it as Floral Hall.

1897
Rotunda

1876
Original
Building

1904
Rotunda
& Hall

Above is a floorplan showing the expansion of Floral Hall over the years. At left, the enlarged Floral Hall, 1904.

In 1905 a young fairgoer skirted near disaster, thanks to a runaway balloon. On Wednesday, September 20, at 3:30 p.m., the balloon operated by Phelps and Burke suddenly slipped its moorings and went sailing off into space, its tether rope having been broken off about 100 feet down from the cage. On board was unsuspecting 15 year-old Floyd Wallace, son of Mrs. John Olmstead of Hunt Street in Oneonta. Floyd worked at

Floyd Wallace

the nearby silk mill when he wasn't spending time near the balloon, which for him had become a fascination.

Several thousand fairgoers watched as the balloon drifted out of sight, fearing that the boy would never be seen alive again. The only individual who seemed unconcerned was the boy's stepfather, Mr. Olmstead. Mr. Olmstead stated that "he guessed the boy would get back all right," and went back to selling peanuts.

As events unfolded, Mr. Olmstead's confidence was apparently justified. Floyd later recounted his thrilling experience; at first he was frightened, but after regaining his composure he immersed himself in the panoramic vistas of hills and valleys blending together. Knowing that he had to force the balloon into a descent, he pulled the valve rope, but it was unresponsive. He then climbed the ropes and with his pocket knife, cut a foot-square hole in the tough silk, which allowed the release of gas, but at a very slow pace.

As the temperature dropped, Floyd buttoned his coat, turned up his collar and hoped for the best. The balloon continued to drift rapidly to the east, and dropped so low that he could see the outline of the hills. Soon the rope was dragging, and about 4:45 p.m. the balloon touched down in a swamp two miles from Summit, in neighboring Schoharie County. Before the balloon was able to rise again, Floyd cut more holes in the silk which allowed more gas to escape. Neighbors came running to help, and soon boy and balloon were taken to Summit, where word was sent home that he was all right. Later he was driven to Richmondville and placed on a train, which returned him to Oneonta at 10:50 p.m. that night. Aside from picking up a chill, Floyd was in good spirits, eager to share his adventure with family and friends. The young man had always been attracted to the balloon, having made several captive ascensions and boasting to friends that he "knew the ropes." It was later determined that the accident was caused by a bystander who pulled on the ropes when it was being drawn in, jamming it against a guide, where it was sheared off.

The Knox Airship

The Fair Managers continually strove to secure new attractions to thrill the fairgoers, and in 1906 they once again outdid themselves. The Knox Airship had created a sensation from coast to coast when it debuted in 1906, one of the first motorized crafts of its kind in the world. The phenomenon was developed by Charles Knox, the man who made a fortune from gelatin sales. In 1890, he developed the world's first pre-granulated gelatin, after watching his wife engaged in the long and difficult process of making it from scratch. Knox experimented until he found a product that was superior to anything on the market, and his gelatin revolutionized gel cooking in America.

Charles Knox

In addition to being an inventor, Charles Knox was an astute marketing agent and became known as the "Napoleon of Advertising." During the 1900 presidential campaign between William Jennings Bryan and William McKinley, Knox got permission from the Commissioner of Highways to hang fifteen political banners over New York City streets with the words, "Hopes To Win" under each candidate and, across the top, "Knox's Gelatin Always Wins." City officials were irate, but Knox had the permit to hang the banners and declined to remove them. This story made every newspaper in New York State and led to Knox acquiring his new title.

In 1906, Charles Knox once again made the front page, this time for promoting his "New Celestial Yacht," an airship he named "Gelatine." Knox appeared in airshows across America, making headlines and breaking records. There was great excitement in Oneonta when the airship arrived the second week in September on a special express car attached to the D&H train. According to the *Oneonta Herald*, "A practical airship, the dream of a century, and to those who had not seen aerial navigation demonstrated, still almost incomprehensible, is in Oneonta, being made ready for daily flights from the fairgrounds during the exposition next week." The airship crew consisted of Earl B. Porsse, Manager; Elmer Vanvranken, Aeronaut; John Smullen, the Hydrogen Man; and Louis Wolie, Mechanical Expert, who also built the framework.

The airship had made three successful flights within the ten days prior to the Fair. The first, from Mr. Knox's residence in Johnstown to Gloversville, a distance of ten miles; the second, it circling Mr. Knox's home ten times; the last at the Fulton County

Fair in Johnstown. Earlier in the year, the ship was at the Portland (Oregon) Exposition, where it made twenty-seven successful flights, including one of thirty-two miles. From there, the ship was taken to Los Angeles, before making the return trip to New York State.

The balloon and its frame were capable of lifting about six hundred pounds. It was powered by a six-horsepower engine, turning a propeller eight feet across. The airship attracted crowds wherever the train stopped along the way, and the *Herald* opined, "This is unquestionably the greatest attraction ever offered at the Oneonta Fair and the flights next week will be events of importance in the history of Oneonta."

The balloon made its initial ascent on Wednesday, September 17, 1906, to the delight of captivated fairgoers. This came after hours of anticipation as the balloon was slowly filled, the metal framing was attached to the balloon with cords, and the necessary sandbags were loaded. Once the preparations were completed, the engine was started, and after minor adjustments, the word was given to release the tethers, and the ship glided skyward. After ascending to a height of 100 feet, the ship outlined a figure eight, then continued up to an altitude of 1,000 feet. After circling the Fairgrounds several times, the ship was brought back to its resting place by throwing out a few handfuls of

The Knox Airship. (Also see the title page for a postcard image.)

sand. As the airship gracefully descended to the ground, it was greeted with cheers and applause from the thousands gathered for the great event.

Piloting the airship was a strenuous endeavor for Mr. Vanvranken. Being the sole person on the ship, he had to simultaneously control the rudder, adjust the engine, and balance the craft by shifting he weight. Upon landing, Mr. Vanvranken was asked if he enjoyed the ride. "Nobody likes it" was his reply. "I go up in airships and balloons because it is my business and it pays me to do it. I feel confidence in myself and in this ship and if I didn't, I certainly would not make another flight." The airship continued to make ascensions for the remaining days of the Fair, always drawing enthusiastic crowds. In 1907 Professor Vanvranken once again entertained fairgoers, this time in an airship he had designed and built himself, with which he accomplished several successful ascensions.

Since the earliest days of the Fair political speeches had become an established tradition, hosting such notables as Teddy Roosevelt. The speaker for 1907 was Governor Charles Evans Hughes, who gave a lengthy speech on the need for everyday citizens to become more involved in government in order to keep politicians from abusing their powers. The governor drew a sharp contrast between our government and the freedoms we enjoy, as opposed to the monarchical administrations of other nations.

New York Governor Charles Evans Hughes addressing the fairgoers from the Roof Garden in 1907.

Fairgoers arriving in carriages.

Power's Performing Elephants.

One of the highlights of the 1908 Fair was a balloon ascension and parachute jump by Floyd Wallace, the young man who three years earlier had enjoyed an unexpected ride in a runaway balloon. A new attraction at this Fair was Power's Performing Elephants, who thrilled the audience with their precision movements.

The political notable in 1908 was Lt. Governor Chanler, who made a brief speech, insisting that he attended the Fair to meet the constituents of his state, not talk politics. After his speech, he met with local business leaders and politicians while touring the Fair and enjoying a luncheon at the Roof Garden restaurant.

Lt. Governor Chanler, center right, with George Wilber, center left (hand on hat).

1910

In many ways 1910 was a landmark year for the Oneonta Fair; the all-time attendance record was set on Tuesday, September 21, and fairgoers were greeted by a magnificent new steel Grandstand and a pair of breathtaking attractions, including the first airplane to take flight in Central New York.

In May 1910, the Fair Managers announced plans to erect a new Grandstand fabricated entirely from steel, to replace the existing wooden structure. The contract was awarded to the Owego Bridge Company, working with plans prepared by Thomas Fogarty and Son of Bath, New York. The Fair Board asserted that once completed, the Grandstand would be "the finest and best to be found upon the grounds of any agricultural society in the state, excepting only the stands upon the State Fairgrounds at Syracuse."

Left: Original grandstand, built in 1893, enlarged in 1897. Dimensions: 30' x 120'; Capacity: 600. Right: New grandstand under construction, 1910. Courtesy of NYSHA.

The dimensions of the new structure were to be 240 by 50 feet deep, resting on concrete walls and pillars. Owego Bridge Company contracted W. F. Kirchoff of Oneonta to do the actual construction. The capacity of the new Grandstand was to be 3,000, five times the capacity of the original structure. The plans included a row of boxes along the front, with a fifteen foot deep concrete paddock running the full length of the stand. The construction price was about $30,000, and work was initiated in late May, with a guaranteed completion date of September 17, 1910. The Grandstand was

Two views of the new Grandstand after completion. (Left: Courtesy of NYSHA.)

placed at a slight angle to afford a better view of the track and infield. Once completed, the new Grandstand complimented the enlarged Floral Hall and further enhanced the Oneonta Fair's reputation as one of the finest in the state.

The Fair opened on Tuesday, September 21, 1910, and by the end of the day a record crowd of 30,000 visitors had filled the grounds, a number that would never be bettered. The incredible influx of fairgoers was a direct result of the sensation brought about by the arrival of the first airplane in Oneonta. In early September, Fair President George Wilber notified the *Oneonta Herald* that he had contracted with aviator Joe Seymour to bring his airplane to the Fair for demonstration flights.

This news spread rapidly through the village, practically guaranteeing a record turnout for the first day. The *Oneonta Herald* confidently stated: "Never in the history of any fair in this section has an attraction caused so much comment as this aeroplane and thousands of people will grasp this opportunity of seeing a "bird-man" for the first time."

On Saturday, September 18, the craft arrived in Oneonta, accompanied by Mr. Seymour, his manager Mr. Larkin, Mr. Wilber, and Joe Seymour's mechanics. After arriving in Oneonta, Joe Seymour and his manager accompanied Mr. Wilber to the Fairgrounds to survey the terrain in anticipation of flights the following week. After assessing the situation, the pilot decided that ascending or landing at the grounds would be unsafe for the crowds, so the decision was made to use the flats on the Kerr Farm across the river, a site which was totally visible from the Fairgrounds.

George Wilber was somewhat disappointed with Joe Seymour's decision, but he agreed that the most important consideration was the safety of the fairgoers. Both men felt that the ideal situation would be to give the aeroplane a prominent location for display, where it could be viewed by the public prior to the flight. A large tent was set up on the Kerr Farm on South Side near the road and visitors were charged ten cents to view what at the time must have seemed like an incredible marvel. Lights were installed in the tent so that the plane could be viewed at night. Seymour's plane was patterned after the craft that was designed and built by Glenn Curtiss, with which he made a successful flight from Albany to New York City. There was some concern on the part of the Fair Managers as to the overall safety of the event, as many in the aviation field had voiced the opinion that it was impossible to conduct flights in hilly areas, in view of the fact that all early flights had been done on flat terrain. Mr. Seymour was not concerned about the hazards, having already made hundreds of flights, in addition to contracting as pilot for the growing movie industry.

The Fairgrounds were packed early in the day, in anticipation of the scheduled flight at 4 p.m. Thousands of people poured into Oneonta from all directions. The Electric City Band ran an excursion from Schenectady carrying 1,000 passengers, while the D&H transported 3,000 from Binghamton and Scranton. A special train was dispatched from Albany with fifteen coaches, and the U&D ran the largest Fair train in its history, with a total of 2,000 passengers on board, and the trolley line ran at full capacity all day. In addition to the thousands who had come by rail, the grounds were jammed with automobiles, a harbinger of things to come.

The other special attraction on opening day was the Golden Globe of Death, appearing at Oneonta for the first time. This death-defying performance involved a female cyclist named CeDora and a 20-foot high steel wire cage painted gold. After circling the inside of the globe on a bicycle at high speeds, CeDora switched to a motorcycle which she propelled across the inside of the cage until she crossed the top upside-down, with one of the male riders standing under her! Throughout her act, CeDora held the large crowd spellbound. This was CeDora's fourth week performing the act since she left the hospital in New York City, where she was confined for eight weeks as a result of an accident sustained while doing the same routine. CeDora had been doing this line of work for four years and said that she had never known a moment of fear. Her assistant, Hector Hadfield, was a young English boy, sixteen years of age. He had done the act for three years and had become an expert.

Other attractions included Daily Brothers Acrobats and Dewar's Animal Circus, which consisted of two ponies, a mule, a dog,

The Golden Globe of Death.

CENTRAL NEW YORK FAIR

ONEONTA, SEPT. 19, 20, 21 and 22, 1910

GRAND FLORAL PARADE
WEDNESDAY and THURSDAY, SEPT. 21 and 22

EXCITING RACES DAILY   LARGE EXHIBITS

THE GREATEST ATTRACTIONS EVER OFFERED

CEDORA

SENSATIONAL ACTS

Globe of Death Act

The best place to see all the features is from a seat in the big steel grand stand.
Come Tuesday—You will want to see the fair daily.

This ad appeared in the Oneonta Star *on September 17, 1910 promoting the two new attractions at the Fair, and recommending the new Grandstand as the best place to see them.*

and revolving table. Also providing entertainment was Meyer and Company's Magic and Illusions and Charles Oakley of the Champlin Stock Company, who performed two solos, "Love Me Deary" and "The Flag of Uncle Sam." The Midway offered the usual side shows, vendors and rides. A yearly favorite was Herman's Popcorn and Homemade Candy, which had been a staple at the Fair for a generation. Another regular at the Fair was Millard and Keenan's Ponies, eagerly anticipated by boys and girls of all ages. One of the most popular booths housed a horse that talked and laughed like a human.

Those who had made the trip were in awe of the new Grandstand, which seemed to dwarf the older structure. The other improvement most appreciated by the visitors was the installation of new ladies and gentlemen lavatories, a great improvement over the existing facilities. The Floral Hall offered an abundance of exhibits in the Ladies Department, including baked goods, quilts, and embroidery. The Relics Department included many unique exhibits, including a bugle used in Napoleon's army, and a deed from the reign of Queen Anne in 1509. The livestock barns were full and several pens had to be enlarged prior to the opening. The largest exhibitor was E. E. Riscey of Walton, who displayed fourteen distinct breeds of swine. The horse show was also the largest in the Fair's history, with most of the entries coming from vicinity farms, and the Poultry Department had twice as many entries as the prior year.

The balloon ascensions were performed by Professor Phelps, who also made the parachute drop. Due to heavy winds, the balloon ascension on Wednesday had to ascend to a higher altitude, and it remained in the air for twenty minutes before touching down five miles from the Fairgrounds. Phelps made a perfect parachute drop, landing on South Mountain, two miles from the Fair.

In spite of the many outstanding attractions, the biggest thrill was yet to come. By mid-afternoon the Fairgrounds were packed with eager fairgoers and the Grandstand was filled to capacity, all anxiously awaiting the first aeroplane to take wing in Oneonta. The flight was scheduled for 4 p.m., so shortly before that time Joe Seymour carefully surveyed the clouds, and then observed that the smoke hung low over the U&D round-house, thereafter deciding that conditions were favorable for a trial flight. The plane was rolled out of the tent and down to a bluff, not far from the river bank, and turned so that it was facing the hills south of the city. A few minor adjustments were made, and then Seymour seated himself at the helm, giving the order for his assistant to spin the propeller. Soon the engine began to purr and the plane gently went aloft, sailing toward the hill at the south. On approaching the highway, midway between the Kerr and the Todd homes, Seymour saw that he could not clear the telephone lines, so he dropped to the earth gliding along for a few hundred feet and then stopping.

The biplane was pulled up to the bluff again and this time it was placed on a higher knoll, further to the east. With this attempt, the craft gracefully lifted itself from the knoll to the delight of the spectators on the Fairgrounds, certain that the plane would clear the telephone lines and sail away toward the hills in the distance. However, as the craft neared the highway, it lost the breeze that had given the needed lift, and it started to sag. At once realizing that he could no longer clear the wires, Seymour pointed the nose downward only to find that two lines of poles made it impossible to miss both of them. He had no alternative and the left side of the ship crashed into the nearest pole, breaking that side in two. The other side veered downward and was also broken in two. Onlookers gasped in horror, fearing the worse. Their fears were unfounded, however, as soon after the crash Joe Seymour was on his feet, gazing at the wreck.

Upon being reached by his crew, Joe's first words were "I've seen worse wrecks than that." He assured the officials that he would repair the plane as quickly as possible and make a flight before leaving Oneonta. Before the engine had cooled, Seymour and his crew began taking an inventory of parts needed to repair the plane. The broken plane was briefly placed on display at the Roof Garden while the inventory was being done. Orders were phoned to New York City for parts and local carpenters were working on the plane the next day. Mr. Seymour and his crew worked well into the night on Wednesday in anticipation of making a flight the following day. In spite of the disappointment, those who witnessed the ascension agreed that the air would be conquered by locomotion even as earth and sea had been.

As the repairs proved to be more extensive than the crew had anticipated, Joe Seymour rescheduled his flight to Saturday. Unfortunately, the weather took a turn for the worse, and with the forecast of rain the entire day, Mr. Seymour was forced to abandon the flight in order to honor an engagement in New Jersey. Although the series of events was a great disappointment for the Oneonta Fair, Joe Seymour was given due credit for his diligence in doing all that was possible to deliver his demonstration.

In spite of the failed flight, those at the 1910 Fair found a great many other diversions, including one of the earliest motorcycle races. There were four entries: Earl

The West End Mission won First Prize for this float in the 1910 Floral Parade.

Fritts, Albert Osborne, and Leroy Crim (all of Colliers) on Indian motorcycles, and Charles Wheat (of Sidney) on a Reading-Standard. The Indian motorcycles took the first three positions. On Wednesday and Thursday, the Floral Parade took place, always the highlight of the Fair. However, for the first time the *Herald* reported that the parade was smaller than the previous year. There were many impressive floats, including one assembled by the City Lunchroom, depicting a miniature dining room; the WCTU float contained so many names of virtues that it was difficult to discern more than a few. The first prize went to the West End Mission for their floral depiction of a yacht surrounded by a dozen young ladies in nautical dress. The parade also included veteran firemen in full dress uniform, and horseback riders dancing to the music of the Electric City Band from Schenectady.

There were two horse races on Wednesday, each with three heats. First prize of $400 was won by "May Girl," owned by Levi Peterson of Honesdale. The last day of the Fair included a horse show, parade of winners, and a free-for-all horse race in which entries did not have to pre-register.

FREE-FOR-ALL RACE AT ONEONTA FAIR

Two views of the new Grandstand filled to capacity.

By the second decade of the 20th century, the automobile had begun to take over the Fairgrounds.

One of the many vendors displaying his wares in a tent set up on the Fairgrounds.

Animal acts were always crowd pleasers at the Fair.

The Subway

After the new Grandstand was completed, an underground subway was installed so that fairgoers were able to walk from the entrance to the Grandstand without crossing the race track, thereby eliminating a major safety concern. The subway was located next to the ticket booth at the head of Fair Street, and it was hailed as the first subway built by a fair in New York State.

The Midway

The Midway area in the center of the race track provided space for amusement rides, food vendors, and business exhibits. In later years much of the area was occupied by automobile and machinery dealers.

THE SECOND DECADE

Over the years the Central New York Fair had adopted a weekly schedule of activities for the four day event. Monday was always registration day, when entries in the various prize categories were processed and assigned to a specific location. Tuesday was Old Home Day and awards day, when prizes for all the departments would be presented. Wednesday hosted the Grand Floral Parade and horse races in addition to special attractions on the Roof Garden. Thursday, the final day of the fair, featured a free-for-all horse race and a parade of the winners in the Floral Parade. Premier attractions, such as balloon ascensions and airplane flights, would usually be presented on all three days.

The 1911 Fair was highlighted by the promise of another attempt to demonstrate flight, this time with a a new aviator, "Ely the bird-man." There was a great deal of apprehension in the crowd, recalling the ill-fated flight of Joe Seymour the previous year. Ely made his first flight at 3:30 p.m. on Tuesday September 19, and as his craft gracefully ascended from the flats on South Side, all concerns were swept aside. At the first sound of the propeller all eyes were turned skyward, both at the Fair and across the city. The plane remained airborne for 20 minutes, making a wide circle over the hills surrounding the Susquehanna Valley, while reaching an altitude of over 500 feet. Spectators were captivated as the plane spiraled and plunged toward the ground, then pulling out of the dive just in time to avert disaster. An unexpected result of the flight involved a flock of doves belonging to a farmer north of the Fairground. Having never seen this strange type of bird, the flock took flight and followed the plane thru some of its maneuvers. The flight on Wednesday attracted even larger crowds, including several hundred congregated around the field on South Side. Mr. Ely did not disappoint spectators, at one point climbing to

Aviator Ely ready for Flight, At Central New York Fair, Oneonta, N. Y.

an altitude of over 1,000 feet. According to the *Herald*: "There are no more daring or more successful aviators in the Country than Mr. Ely."

In addition to the excitement generated by the first successful airplane flights, the Roof Garden attractions were some of the best ever offered, including Mazetti's Acrobats, Louis Stanton's Trunk Escapes, the Rex Comedy Animal Circus, and Hutton's Hippodrome on the track, featuring chariot races and riderless trotters. Inside the exhibition building, the Art Department offered a collection of several hundred photos of old Oneonta, provided by William H. Wilson of the city's post office. Oneonta merchants provided an abundance of commercial items; in addition to the usual stoves and sewing machines, there were demonstrations of the new Lauson Frost King gasoline engines.

The Floral Parade included 39 entries, a substantial increase over the 1910 event. Mrs. Edith Bates won first prize for lady horseback riders, while the single team prize went to Mrs. W. Johnson and the double to George Cook. The first prize for trade union floats went to "Rock of Ages," which was decorated by the Ladies Society of Plains Church. Second and third prizes went to the W.C.T.U. floats, with one prize going to the young ladies branch. First prize for decorated ladies bicycles went to Zada Lockwood. There were four classes of floats for non-individual entries: school, business, fire department, and trade union. Trade union floats included church, social groups, political, and benevolent agencies. Individual entries included bicycle, horseback, single horse or team and double team carriages.

Floral Parade winner - Ladies horseback.

Floral Parade winner - Single team.

Floral Parade winner - Double team.

Floral Parade winner - Decorated bicycle.

On Tuesday the 2:12 Trot and the 2:15 Pace were both won by "Town Director," owned by Clark and Patterson. On Wednesday the best 2 of 3 was won by "Castor," belonging to O.W. Welch. There was some disappointing news on the last day of the Fair when Mr. Ely reluctantly canceled his flights due to excessive winds. The day was not without excitement, however, thanks to an accident in the motorcycle race; Willard Otten lost control of his machine on the turn and slammed into the wall, throwing him from the machine. Willard was not seriously injured and was taken to his home in East End to recuperate. The race was won by Earl Fritts of Oneonta.

There was a wide variety of entries in the Cattle Department: first prize in Short-horns went to E.L. Titis of Sidney Center; first in Brown Swiss to L.E. Higbee of Trout Creek, and first in Red Polls went to Fred Terpenning of West One-

Cattle barns.

onta. The Packer farm of Portlandville took first prize in French Canadians, and F.E. Stevens won first prize in French Canadians and Normandys, with one bull weighing in at over 2,800 pounds.

Prior to the 1912 Fair, the Managers made it known that they were investing a total of $10,000 in prizes and attractions, hoping to make it the most memorable week in the Fair's history. Ads were placed in railroad stations throughout Central New York describing the wide variety of attractions, including not one, but two aviators making flights above the grounds! Arrangements were made to secure new performers on the Roof Garden, including the Carl Dammon Family, considered to be the best acrobatic troupe in Europe. Also engaged for Fair Week was the Fillis Family, the world's most well-known equestrian performers, with a program including dancing and leaping horses. James Fillis, leader of the troupe, was the personal horse trainer for the Czar of Russia.

Of course the main attraction was once again the daring "birdmen." By noon on Tuesday the anticipation must have been near unbearable, but the spectators soon found out that the air show was worth waiting for. The first flight was made by aviator Hemstraught at 1 p.m., keeping his plane aloft for a full 30 minutes. After ascending from Kerr Flats on South Side, he piloted the plane toward West Davenport, then banked left and pointed the nose toward Emmons and circled the Fairground before crossing over the Normal School on the way to West End, then finally he banked left again and returned to the landing field, with applause so great that it was probably heard at the Kerr Farm. Wednesday's flights were canceled due to inclement weather, but on Thursday aviator Walter Johnson thrilled those on the ground when he swooped down over the Fairgrounds so low that many thought he would scrape the rooftops.

In spite of the attention given to the fliers, an editorial in the *Oneonta Herald* indicated there was growing concern over the automobile's impact on Fair attendance: "The Fair will certainly surpass all previous exhibitions and residents of the city should prepare to keep an open house for relatives and friends from away and all residents of the section should plan to visit the Fair one or more days as it cannot be seen satisfactorily in one day." Many loyal fairgoers returned year after year, and looked forward to familiar institutions such as Brown's Lunch Room under the Roof Garden and Herman's Hot

Candy and Popcorn. By 1912 Herman had been a regular at the Central New York Fair for over 20 years. Every summer during fair season Herman left his shop at Folman's Pavilion in Coney Island to do the Upstate fairs, much to the delight of fairgoers young and old, who savored his delicious treats.

In 1913 the Oneonta fairgoers were entertained by a home-grown aviator, Earl Fritts. Earl had been a Fair regular for many years driving in the motorcycle races, and he now employed his mechanical aptitude in constructing his own flying machine. The Fair Managers had contracted with a second flier, Frank Burnside, who was to fly his airplane the full distance from Bath, New York to Oneonta, but his flight was canceled due to mechanical problems. The Managers continued to offer a wide variety of attractions, adopting the slogan, "A dollar's worth for a quarter," the admission price. As the second decade of the 20th century progressed, the dynamic of American leisure activities was rapidly changing. Americans were on the move, thanks to the automobile. fairgoers were more likely to drive from Albany or Binghamton, enjoy the attractions at the fair and return home in the evening, instead of

EARL V. FRITTS, ONEONTA'S FAMOUS AVIATOR
He will make daily flights, weather permitting, at the Oneonta Fair

Race Entries for Oneonta Fair

Exceptionally large list of well-known horses entered, assuring exciting races. Never in the history of the Central New York Fair has the list of entries been larger than for the annual meet next week, and in the list of fast trotters and pacers are many which are known to those fond of racing to be game and hard to beat. About ten of this year's entries are of horses owned outside the state.

The list of entries follows, and will prove one of the best drawing cards of the fair:

Official Entry List—Oneonta Union Agricultural Society

Sept. 15, 16, 17, 18, --- 1913

TUESDAY SEPTEMBER 16

CLASS NO. 1—2.14 Pace and 2.10 Trot. Purse $100.

Oneonta Herald, *September 1913.*

spending a week in Oneonta as was done in earlier days. As evidence of the visitors' changing habits, the *Herald* reported: "The crowd was a normal one with no large excursions from distant points and the enclosure within the race track was filled with motor cars and vehicles of all kinds."

The 1914 Fair saw a near-record attendance, estimated at over 25,000, and the proliferation of automobiles was even more evident. No fliers were scheduled and the management reverted to the balloon ascension and parachute jump, probably as a cost-cutting measure. The highlight of the four-day event was a speech delivered by Navy Under-Secretary Franklin Delano Roosevelt, who was running for United States Senate. Mr. Roosevelt praised President Wilson's handling of the situation in Mexico and stressed the importance of selecting an Upstate man for the Senate seat.

Even though the program was lacking a "birdman," there was an abundance of attractions on the Roof Garden. The most elaborate entertainment was delivered by Carranda's Animal Act, featuring an elephant, a dancing horse, a pair of zebras, and two large dogs. The elephant seemed to possess almost human intelligence, walking on two feet, dancing and leading one of the zebras around the ring. A close second went to D'Artagnan's Lion Equestrian Act, which amazed spectators with the incredible combination of a lion riding a horse while jumping through hoops!

Perhaps the most anticipated act was "Daredevil Long," a performer who had gained enough popularity that the Fair Board had been trying for three years to secure his appearance. What was amazing about his act was that he performed all his stunts while standing on his head! This included walking downstairs, skating down an incline, and jumping five feet from one platform to another. He also swung upside down on a trapeze while taking a drink and smoking a cigarette. Another new attraction for 1915 was Oliver the High Diver. Oliver dove backward 104 feet into 54 inches of water, while at the same time his dog dove 50 feet from the same ladder, both landing in the tank at the same time.

Left: An unidentified animal act. (Courtesy of NYSHA.) Right: 1915 International Harvester farm tractor.

The star feature in the machinery department was the Fair's first farm tractor, an International Harvester, which boasted that it would run on any type of combustible fuel and could turn on a 20 foot circle. The tractor retailed for $675 and was marketed by Murdock Brothers of Oneonta.

By 1915 auto dealers were taking up a good deal of the commercial section, and Oneonta dealer Arthur M. Butts had new models of Chandlers and Oaklands on display. Other commercial exhibitors included Brown and Tucker's selection of stoves, and James Munn's musical instruments.

In 1916 the Oneonta Fair engaged Lawrence Brown, the most famous pilot in America. Lawrence was the country's first "flying ace," prior to the term gaining popularity in World War One. Lawrence Brown resided in Los Angeles and began flying in 1914, obtaining one of the state's first pilot licenses. His competence as a flier spread throughout the southwest and into Mexico, where his abilities came to the attention of the country's new president, Venustiano Carranza. After the Mexican revolution of 1913, a power struggle ensued between Carranza and outlaw Pancho Villa. Villa commanded a large army, but Carranza hoped that utilizing the airplane as a tactical weapon might give him the advantage. This was not a totally new concept, as Italy had been the first nation to employ the plane in combat during the conquest of Cyrenaica and Tripolitania in 1911-12.

Christofferson biplane.

Beginning in February 1915, Brown made 3-5 bombing and reconnaissance runs a week in a Christofferson biplane, ceasing flights in August due to a bout with typhus which sent him back to Los Angeles for recuperation. While flying in Mexico he was a member of the Carranza Serial Scouts, and it was not long before he was appointed chief of the squadron. Brown was assigned the duty of doing battle with Villa's limited air force, flying Curtis Pusher airplanes that had been smuggled into the country. Lawrence Brown's daredevil flying gave him a definite advantage over the enemy, flying circles around Villa's planes. After downing a total of 23 fliers, Villa referred to the Serial Scouts as the "Gringo Devils." Brown's flying partner Mickey McGuire was captured and executed by the rebels, but Brown continued flying missions until his return to Los Angeles in August. After a brief recuperation he served as instructor at the Glen Martin Flying School until the summer of 1916, when he went to work for the Standard Company of Plainfield, New Jersey as a test pilot. In June he performed his first stunt show at Mineola on Long Island, executing loops and spirals to prepare himself for the fair circuit in fall.

After a vigorous buildup in the local papers, everyone was eager to witness flights by the California ace. Lawrence Brown arrived in Oneonta on Tuesday, prepared to fly the next two days; the only problem was that his plane did not arrive when he did.

Brown had just finished an engagement in Ottawa, Ontario, Canada, and the plane was on a freight train headed to the United States. He immediately contacted the express company by wire and found that the plane was detained at the border due to a problem with the freight car carrying it. Mr. Brown ordered the shipper to break locks and do whatever was necessary to get the shipment moving. This situation was a disaster for both the fairgoers and Superintendent George Wilber, who had contracted with Brown to make flights on two days during the week.

By Wednesday Brown was wired that the problem had been solved and the shipment should be in Oneonta by Thursday. However, this was not to be the case, as he was notified late Wednesday that the shipment was being held up in Syracuse for the same problem with the freight car. At this point the pilot worked frantically with both the New York Central and the Delaware and Hudson to resolve the problem. Mr. Brown was very concerned about delivering on his commitment, and he was under pressure from George Wilber to honor his contract.

The plane finally arrived in Oneonta on Thursday, but there was not enough time to get the craft ready for flights before Friday. Since Mr. Brown had contracted to make two flights, he went out at 5 p.m., and then made a second flight shortly thereafter. The crowd soon learned that the event was worth waiting for, as the ace gave them a spectacular show of loops, upside-downs, and spirals, and he even included a demonstration of aerial bombing with dummy bombs. In an interview after the flights, Brown described the method of bombing in his Mexican battles. In a single-seat plane the bomb was tied to the side of the fuselage and the pilot cut the rope with a knife when he was over the target. In a two-seater the passenger would drop the bomb through a hole in the floor between his legs.

Besides the disappointment over Lawrence Brown's delay, there were a lot of unhappy schoolchildren in Oneonta who were banned from the Fair due to an outbreak of infantile paralysis, which had caused the Morris Fair to cancel completely. The adults who attended were pleased to find a number of new attractions, including the Montrose Colonial Acrobats and Professor Johnson, a slack-wire artist who amazed spectators with his ability to jump through hoops while on the wire. A new attraction was the Hurmandos Circus, billed as a miniature Barnum & Bailey; ponies and dogs were paired up in an amazing performance with one pair jumping rope while the other pair danced to "Turkey in the Straw." The animals then took turns trying to stay on a revolving table, with the goat and pony winning the contest.

Not to be outdone, the next act was "Big Jim," the rolling skating bear. After going through a dance repertoire including the Turkey Trot, Tango, and Hula, "Big Jim" engaged in a wrestling match with grappler Maurice Fishman, *aka* "Kid Green" of New York City, with the bear coming out on top. The week concluded with a lavish wedding, which had always been a very popular event at the annual fair. After a luncheon under the Roof Garden, the couple jumped in their auto and headed to the Adirondacks for the honeymoon. Since the delay in Lawrence Brown's aerial performance pushed the fair into Friday, the management decided to continue with a five day event after 1916.

Bleriot monoplane.

The 1917 Fair brought a new birdman to Oneonta, John Domanjoz, who piloted a Bleriot monoplane, dazzling the spectators with loops, upside downs and corkscrews, all in rapid succession. The Fair was well attended allowing visitors a temporary diversion from the realities of war that now involved the United States. The Delaware and Hudson added coaches to the Fair Week trains, although there were no special excursions. Replacing some of the passenger traffic were hundreds of automobiles jamming the city streets. The grounds offered the usual side show rides and vendors, including the old standby, Herman's of Coney Island.

A popular attraction in the commercial section was the introduction of the Linn Tractor, produced locally in Morris, New York. The Linn was promoted as an all-purpose hauler, capable of drawing several trailers equally well over hard ground or swamp. C.C. Miller demonstrated his hot air furnace billed as "the hottest thing on earth." The versatile unit would burn wood, coal or coke. By 1917, the Suffragettes had become well-established at the Fair, providing a large tent with easy chairs, coaches and cold drinks for weary fairgoers. On the second day of the Fair, Frederick R. Losey of Columbia University gave an impassioned speech advocating votes for women.

On Wednesday, September 18, 1918, the City Page of the *Oneonta Herald* carried side-by-side stories that could not be further apart. Next to a glowing description of the Central New York Fair was a report on the arrest of a German sympathizer at the Hathaway House on Broad Street, a stark reminder that the nation was at war. The arrest actually rescued the sympathizer from an angry mob of about thirty men who chased him out into the street. The *Herald*

The Linn Tractor.

speculated that he would be handed over to the U.S. Court, where he could explain his unpatriotic stand.

As for the Fair, the first day began with a cold mist, but by using brush drags the crews were able to prepare the track for a race at 3 p.m. According to the *Herald*, the crowd was not large, but seemed more interested in amusement rides than merchant's exhibits. The Roof Garden once again provided a variety of entertainments, including "Little Hip," the trained elephant, and "Napoleon the Great," a trained baboon whose antics entertained the crowds for all three days. Animal combination acts were very popular at the Fair and Tunelli's Trained Comedy Circus attempted to outdo anything that the crowd had seen. The act included four ponies, a trio of trained dogs, a small monkey, and a mule.

Giving the Fair an international flavor, the five McClarons performed in kilts and displayed their talents with bagpipes and drums, rendering such classics as "Bonnie Scotland." Rounding out the program were the Three Rianos, dressed as animals and engaging in a combination of acrobatics and slapstick comedy. Possibly by this time the airplane had lost its novelty, as the "Birdman" had been replaced by the return of Dr. Phelps and his balloon ascension, accompanied by a parachute drop. The Floral Parade for Wednesday was postponed until Thursday, due to a prolonged downpour which also necessitated the rescheduling of the horse races to Thursday and Friday. The unexpected rainstorm was a benefit to downtown theaters and businesses, giving the fairgoers a refuge from the inclement weather.

The *Herald*'s account of the 1919 Fair was subdued but enthusiastic, estimating the crowd at 15,000 on the first day, which would be the highest attendance of the week. Roof Garden performers included acrobats Arnold and Florence, in addition to the Whirling Azomas. The customary animal act was not overlooked, as the Barzac Circus performed an unusual horse and dog routine. With each passing year, the Fairgrounds gave more and more space to auto dealers. New models for 1919 included Nash, Buick, Overlands, and Sterns-Harding. Fine music was provided throughout the week by the Oneonta City Band, under the direction of James Keeton, Jr.

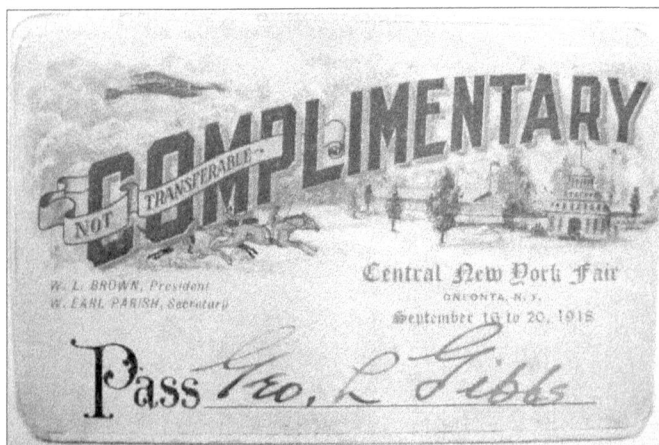

COMPLIMENTARY
NOT TRANSFERABLE

W. L. BROWN, President
W. EARL PARISH, Secretary

Central New York Fair
ONEONTA, N.Y.
September 18 to 20, 1918

Pass *Geo. L Gibbs*

GREAT

Central New York Fair

Our Fair is Your Fair

THE FIRST PRESIDENT OF THE CENTRAL NEW YORK FAIR

Oneonta, New York
September 17, 18, 19, 20, 21

Nineteen Seventeen

Page from the official program of the 1917 Fair, featuring George Wilber.

THE FINAL YEARS

A week prior to the 1920 Central New York Fair the *Oneonta Herald* ran a telling editorial titled, "Who sees the Fair?" According to the writer, some individuals thought of the Fair only as an agricultural exhibit, while to others it was purely entertaining or educational. The *Herald* advanced the argument that it is actually all three and should be enjoyed as such. In short, the Fair offered something for everyone, and with the Delaware and Hudson offering discounted rates for Fair week, all who were able should attend and support a local enterprise celebrating its 48th year.

The 1920 Oneonta Fair enjoyed a week of good weather, and President George Wilber estimated that the crowds were the largest since the Fair had been extended to five days. The Floral Parade was led by Fair Superintendent S.B. Gardner and the Company G Band, a precedent established with the first parade. There were three big horse races and a good selection of exhibitors, including C.C. Miller, who displayed water systems and milkers; A.H. Murdock's International Farm Machinery, and Lane's Electric, merchandising the latest in electrical appliances. New items on display included gramophones, cameras, and flush toilets.

A special feature for 1920 was the Endicott-Johnson Band and Chorus, whose eighty members gave a concert in a specially erected stand east of Floral Hall. The concert was conducted by former Oneontan Harold Albert, and many old friends were pleased to welcome him back to his home town. The band performed many old favorites, including "Swanee River," "Hiawatha's Love Song," and "Let the Rest of the World Go By."

One of the most popular exhibits in the commercial section was the Chenango Camp Trailer, which was manufactured in Norwich, New York. It was marketed as "the simplest, most compact and best equipped camping outfit on the market."

Prior to the 1921 opening, the Fairgrounds infield had been reorganized to provide more parking space for automobiles, and a force of New York State Troopers had been employed to administer the parking area. The *Oneonta Star* expressed concern over the appearance of several "palmists" on the grounds, who were considered to be nothing more than roving gypsies. Many of these people were turned away before they were able to set up. The star performer in the horse races was "May Daphine" of Stamford, owned and driven by Dr. W.H. Wheeler. "May" won both the 2:30 Pace and the 2:26 Trot, while the 2:24 Trot was won by "Baron Deforest," owned by B.B. Jermyn of Scranton.

The 1921 Fair featured a thrilling new attraction never before seen in Oneonta, or elsewhere in the east. In August it was announced that the Fearless Grecos Stunt Driver Show would be performing on the Oneonta track throughout the week. The crowds were breathless as autos shot up ramps and did somersaults over another vehicle on the track below. On Wednesday, one of the cars lost control, crashed into the wall and overturned. The crowd was relieved when the young lady climbed uninjured out of the overturned vehicle. The cars were well padded and specially constructed to prevent injuries. Although the stunt car ads stated that it was "the most thrilling and sensational spectacle ever conceived," the *Star* commented that, like the rumored death of Mark Twain, the statement was greatly exaggerated.

The *Star* lamented that interest in the traditional Fair attractions, such as liberal arts, cattle, and poultry were waning, while visitors spent more time on amusement rides, including the merry-go-round, Ferris wheel, and the seaplanes, a new ride which was filled to capacity throughout the Fair. The *Star* also suggested that the vaudeville acts should be moved away from the Roof Garden so that the crowds would not spend the entire day in the Grandstand at the expense of the exhibits on the ground. The car show continued to expand, with the Oneonta Sales Company offering a full display of Ford cars, trucks, and tractors. Fred Van Wie debuted the Cole automobile, offering a coupe, sedan, and touring car.

On July 13, 1922, George I. Wilber passed away, bringing to an end the dynasty that had brought the Oneonta Fair to life. The Fair had been struggling for years against the competition from other fairs and the changing lifestyle wrought by the automobile. Wilber was the principal stockholder in the Agricultural Society, but eventually his stock would be purchased by Vice President D.F. Keyes, effectively putting him in charge of a dying entity whose years were numbered.

The 1922 Fair opened to a smaller than usual crowd on Tuesday, September 19. The weather was very chilly and rain threatened throughout the day. The *Star* noted that there were less side shows and vendor booths than in former years, although the vacant spaces were quickly occupied by new dealers in "Automobile Row," with many new makes appearing

George Wilber

yearly. The Roof Garden attractions included Four American Aces, an acrobatic team that impressed the crowds with maneuvers on horizontal bars. Next up was an act dubbed "Foolish, Wise and Reckless," comprised of a female tumbler, a trained dog, and a mule. Spectators were invited to attempt riding the mule, but none were successful.

The headliner act, Olympia Desvall and Company, did not receive a favorable response from the audience. The *Star* observed that the act did not have the ability to thrill the crowd and hold their interest. Other acts included the Bounding Kirkillos, a juggling and tumbling act, and Poodles and Dottie, a man and woman who performed a number of balancing stunts.

The flier for 1922 was P.R. Moore, who had served with the Royal Flying Corps during the war. Mr. Moore made his first flight on Tuesday at 4 p.m., but there was so much activity at the Roof Garden that some spectators were not aware of the plane. When the Managers were made aware of this situation, it was decided to make the flights directly across the valley from the Grandstand on Thursday.

Both horse races were won by "Silky Mack," owned by H. M. Stanford of Oneonta.

Apparently there was some good-natured kidding among the Fair's auto dealers. Dan Sherman commented about the brush drag pulled by a Ford auto to smooth the track, "Another insult heaped upon the Ford," to which Mr. Warren of Oneonta Sales replied, "Another demonstration of the practical ability of the Ford." The *Star* noted that although there were 55 horses in the barns, there were only four starters for each event, possibly an indication that owners were preserving the best animals for other venues. The reporter questioned the situation: "Somehow, horsemen have an intuition as to when it is wise to have a horse lame or suffering from lumbago and only four starters appear."

The 1923 Fair opened to good weather and an average crowd on Tuesday, September 19. According to the *Herald* there was a marked increase of vendors on the grounds, in addition to over 20 auto dealers. The Company G Band, who had recently won first prize at the State Fair, provided musical entertainment throughout the week. A new attraction was Doctor Wood the Beeman. The Doctor gave a brief lecture on bees and the benefit of honey, then did a few stunts inside a cage filled with bees. His performance was somewhat limited, however; he had traveled from a fair in Canada and his personal swarm had been held up at the Canadian border so he had to purchase another swarm in Binghamton. Due to the inconvenience he was prevented from doing his usual stunts, swarming the bees into his hat and making a beard form bees.

The headline act was the Six Stella Sisters, an acrobatic troupe. Unfortunately, the six ladies had come from the same fair in Canada as Doctor Wood and their luggage was detained at the border, so they had to improvise costumes. In spite of this problem, the young ladies from Europe gave the crowds an exceptional performance, including unforgettable tumbling and balancing maneuvers. The Peterson Trio, two young women and a clown, delivered an outstanding acrobatic routine, which included one of the young ladies hanging by her teeth. The last performance in the program was given by the Royal Trio, two men and a lady performing stunts on ladders.

Automobile Row continued to grow; Oneonta Sales Company provided the largest display and garnered the most attention. On exhibit were coupes, sedans, and touring cars, ranging in price from $410 to $785. Fred Van Wie was offering the Chevrolet, which featured valve-in-head motors. He displayed coupes equipped with wire wheels, and a number of truck models. The Oneonta Buick company displayed both 4- and 6-cylinder models, and one 6-cylinder model was kept running all day to demonstrate the engine's low vibration. To dramatize this claim a spike was balanced on the radiator cap and two pencils were balanced on the engine block for the duration of the day. Also in auto row were Paige and Jewett autos, presented by C.H. Bennett of Otego, and Maxwells and Chalmers, displayed by the Thompson Motor Company.

The City of Oneonta held a winter car show for several years at the Armory, but after it was discontinued more dealers took advantage of the Fair to showcase their vehicles. In addition to the usual autos, new makes such as Dodge, Hupmobile, Overland, and Willys-Knight had made their appearance. A newcomer for 1923, the Wilber

Automobile Row.

Motor Sales Company, displayed Packard, Hudson, and Essex, while other first-timers included Oldsmobile, Franklin, and Studebaker. The auto business was spawning accessory sales, and there were dealers hawking Socony motor oil, Gould batteries, and Gabriel snubbers, the forerunner of shock absorbers.

Cover of the 1924 program.

In 1924 the Fair management proclaimed that they had exceeded any previous exhibition in securing the most outstanding attractions available in the northeast. The first Roof Garden performance was given by the Comedy Riding School, and it appeared to be a hit with the crowd. The next act was the Vardoli Brothers, a highly acclaimed acrobatic troupe who had recently completed a world tour. The Brothers performed an outstanding series of feats on the trapeze and high bar, catching each other by the feet high above the grounds. Also appearing were Dekoch and Company, a trained dog act and the Colonial Belles, a group of female accordion players who entertained the audience with popular and jazz music.

Rounding out the 1924 Fair was the traditional balloon ascension and parachute drop that, by this time, had taken the place of the "birdmen," a spectacle which had run its course at the Oneonta Fair. In order to cut expenses, the Floral Parade was discontinued prior to the 1924 event.

In 1924 the Fair Managers arranged for a special attraction; the Troop C State Troopers from Sydney had agreed to perform their regimen of precision equine drills. As the last day of the Fair progressed, however, the troopers met with unexpected duty. Three men at the Fair had been under surveillance since the opening, due to suspicious activity. The special Fair police had received a tip from Lorenzo Wayman of Ashland that $140 had been lifted from his hip pocket on Wednesday afternoon. Wayman said he believed that the money was taken when he was jostled while standing on the track in front of the Grandstand. He stated that the money was pinned in his pocket and that about fifteen minutes later he noticed the money and the pin were gone.

On Wednesday Officer D.D. Brown of the Special Police noted three men walking around the grounds and "boxing" a man between them. Brown followed the three around the crowd watching the inflation of the balloon, where he saw them close on another man. He was joined by Officer Ralph Wykoff, and Brown told Wykoff that he had observed one of the men withdraw a black object from the victim's hip pocket while his two accomplices crowded in closely to conceal what was happening. At this point, Brown and Wykoff collared the three suspects, which brought on a fight involving all five men. Officer Brown was kicked in the back by another man, who was apparently a friend of the pickpockets. During the melee, one of the men broke away, and the officers started for the gate in a running struggle with the other two men.

State Trooper Leo O'Hanley was standing on the Roof Garden and heard the ruckus, so he jumped to the ground to assist the other officers. The suspect who had broken away was found at the gate and all three men were arrested and taken to the city jail. The three men arrested were identified as Charles McCann of Troy, Max Stern of Albany, and John Preller of New York City. When searched, McCann had $129 in cash, a sack of morphine and a hypodermic needle. Stern was found to have $118 and a "dope kit"for using the morphine, and Preller was in possession of $103 and a bag of morphine.

The police were still suspicious of the three "dope addicts," so another search was done in the cell. Officers ordered Stern to take off his clothes and at that point, another bag of drugs were found in his underwear. Having been discovered, Stern got into a fight with the officers, while attempting to dump the drugs into a wash bowl and destroy them. Stern kicked Trooper O'Hanley in the hip, after which O'Hanley pinned him to the floor. All three men were charged with numerous crimes by the City Attorney, and Trooper O'Hanley went back to demonstrating his expertise on horseback.

The 1925 Fair was once again highlighted by the Troop C Rodeo, although there was a minor bit of drama when one of the steeds refused to jump through the hoops. According the *Star* reporter, the Roof Garden entertainment was the best available since there were no fliers. The opening act was the two Lamarrs, who performed acrobatics with chairs and bars. They were followed by the three Waltons, a triple bar act. Next came the three Tornato Girls, contortionists and slack-wire walkers, and they were followed by the Original Baggage Smashers, a comedy act. The most popular performance was given by France and Lapoll, a highly-involved balancing act. As in 1922, many of the horses did not start in the race.

The Floral Hall exhibits seemed to lack the luster of previous years. A display by two Oneonta florists presented the proper etiquette for decorating an informal dinner table, and the Relics Department had assembled a collection of Chinese artifacts, including curios, carvings and laces. The one segment of the Fair that continued to prosper was Automobile Row, which now encompassed almost the entire south end of the Midway. As usual, Oneonta Sales Company consumed the most space, showcasing a Fordson Tractor for the first time. New additions for 1925 were the Hudson, Essex, and the Larrabie Truck.

A vacant Midway in later years.

Visitors to the Oneonta Fair in 1926 had no idea they were partaking of the great yearly event for the last time. The *Oneonta Herald* was very positive in its assessment of the opening, proclaiming that as an agricultural exhibition, it surpassed anything in previous years. In addition, the Floral Hall exhibits were described as the best in recent memory, and the Midway offered an abundance of vendors, rides and side shows.

The Roof Garden program began with the five Janslos, an acrobatic troupe. They were followed by Miss Bingham, the "Venus of the Air," performing aerial feats on rings and ropes. The three Kirkillos returned with table and pedestal acrobatics, and the closing acts were the five Avelons on a double tight wire, and the three Bobs, who offered up a comedy clown act. The new additions to Automobile Row for 1926 included Chrysler and Auburn. New products in the commercial section included Cooper Tires, Frigidaire Refrigerators, and Clar-A-Dyne Radios.

Ironically, as 1926 was the year that the Central New York Fair would cease to exist, it was also the year that the Morris Fair would offer a new attraction that would create a sensation and establish a tradition that would draw spectators to the track for over half a century. On Wednesday, September 22, the Grandstand was packed in anticipation of what could be considered the track's first stock car race. There was a total of six races and six cars were entered, and the drivers found themselves negotiating a combination of blinding dust and slick turns with half-dried puddles. The best time on the half-mile track was clocked by Bill Rupp in an Auburn Special, at 35.2 seconds. Rupp held the State record for a half-mile dirt track, doing 32 seconds flat at Altamont Race Track.

Finishing close behind Rupp was Bob Paige in a Dodge, and James Ewers in a Chevrolet. J.L. Hankinson of Kansas City was brought in to serve as race starter, and he kept the race under control with his collection of various colored flags. All the races were close, with one heat being decided by a few inches, and the drivers pushed their machines to over 60 mph. The crowds loved the excitement, and the auto races would become a yearly event, with the Morris race track eventually evolving into the Mid-State Speedway.

The end finally came on April 21, 1927, with Oneontans waking up to the *Star* headline, "To discontinue Oneonta Fair - grounds to be plotted and sold." According to the article, the Central New York Fairgrounds, which embraced about sixteen acres, had been sold and was already subdivided for building lots. After the proposal was ratified by the stockholders, the lots were offered for sale on May 5 by the Fair Society. The development was to yield over one hundred lots, and the promoters believed that their proximity to the business center and the excellent drainage of the terrain would create a demand for the lots and sales would be brisk. The development was to be known as Belmont Park, and the track would be straightened and regraded and given the name Belmont Circle. This street would be the primary artery of the new section, and Hudson Street, which terminated at the east end of the Fairgrounds, would be extended to the grounds to the west end of Floral Hall, and then curve west to join Fair Street near the entrance to the Fairgrounds. Fair Street was to be extended east through the ticket stand and join Belmont Circle above the viaduct under the race track. The lots were arranged so that none would have less than 50 feet of frontage, and the lots on the outside of the circle would not be as deep as those in the interior, many of which would have depths of 80 to 100 feet. The initial plot map showed a total of 116 lots.

At a stockholders meeting on the evening of April 20, D.F. Keyes, who held a controlling interest in the association, stated that at the present time this seemed like the best direction for the Board to pursue. He stated that the patronage of the Fair had not been maintained and public interest in the Fair was waning. Since the advent of the automobile, it had ceased to be a commercial asset to the city, while the expense of maintenance and operation had continued to increase. To further strengthen his case, Mr. Keyes pointed out that there was a shortage of desirable building lots in the city, which had led to construction outside of the corporate limits, while the Fairgrounds had continued to be tax-exempt.

Mr. Keyes estimated that within a few years the new development would present an assessed value of at least $300,000, which would bring $12,000 to $14,000 into the city treasury, and the Belmont Park proposal would result in the construction of many new homes in the city that would otherwise be erected elsewhere, with an increase in assessable property. Mr. Keyes and his associates summarized their argument, stating confidently that the property would have far greater value to the city as a residential neighborhood than as a Fair. The *Star* article then reminisced about the Oneonta Fair's legacy and how it was intertwined with the dedication of George I. Wilber, who coined the slogan, "a dollar's worth for twenty five cents." The article also recalled how the yearly event would draw crowds from Schenectady, Scranton, Wilkes-Barre, and Kingston, filling the city with visitors for a week, and providing the merchants with a very profitable five days of business. All this changed after the automobile became predominant, allowing visitors to come in the afternoon for the races and Fair attractions and return home.

As a footnote, it was revealed that the Oneonta Union Agricultural Society had recently acquired a large tract of land in the Oneonta Plains, near the Country Club, for possible development. However, the lack of sufficient income from the Fair in recent years made it very unlikely that efforts would be made to develop another Fair site. It was estimated that the cost of moving the Grandstand alone would be $15,000, and the expense of erecting buildings and grading a race track would be totally out of proportion to the financial return to the City. The property at The Plains would eventually be developed into an airport by Mr. Keyes.

In closing, the reporter was philosophical regarding the fact that there would be many regrets that the the Fair was to become a thing of the past, but that the residents of Oneonta would still have the County Fair at Cooperstown and the popular Morris

Fair to enjoy in the summer. It was noted that in addition to the value in real estate, the Fair Board possessed a cash balance of $50,000, which would be divided among the stockholders.

By May 5 the *Star* reported that wrecking operations were underway at the Fairgrounds, and it was expected that by July 1 most of the grading for the new lots and streets would be completed. The cattle sheds were being torn down and the lumber was being sold at $20 per 1,000 feet, while the tin roofs were selling at $1 per running foot. Mr. Keyes initially planned to leave Floral Hall standing as a business enterprise if a potential owner was willing to buy several adjacent lots and build on them. The large barn at the Fairgrounds entrance would be torn down to allow for the extension of Fair Street to Belmont Circle. No decision had been made on the disposition of the large Grandstand, as the City had expressed an interest in moving it to the ball field at Neahwa Park, although the $15,000 cost of moving it there would probably be prohibitive. The remaining buildings, with the exception of the chicken house and the barns near the railroad, were to be torn down, but eventually these buildings and Floral Hall would also be dismantled.

Speaking with regards to a July 4th celebration at the Fairgrounds, Mr. Keyes told reporters: "It seems almost impossible to hold the 4th of July celebration in the Fairgrounds, for by July 1st the track and property will be taken up and regraded. This work has already started near Sand Street, where a force of men are cutting out the hill section. The dirt is being placed on the extension of Hudson Street, which is on low ground."

Arrangements were made with Fred Van Wie to sell off the lots after the property was graded, and digging for sewers had been initiated. It was stated that lots would be supplied with gas, electricity, and city water, and the lots would sell for $1,000 and up. The grading work was being done by W.F. Kirchoff, under the direction of Engineer Frank M. Gurney.

In late May of 1927, a proposal to resurrect the Fair was advanced by Mr. D F. Keyes. The proposal stated that Mr. Keyes would donate the steel Grandstand, valued at $25,000, if the City would remove it in three months. In response to the offer, a group of Oneonta citizens formed a committee to explore the possibility of organizing an annual fair or industrial exposition that would offer amusement features similar to the Central New York Fair, to be held in the fall of the year.

The site under consideration by the Committee was a large island adjacent to Neahwa Park, which would later be known as Webb Island. The island had been deeded to the City by Dr. Morris and was undeveloped. While there were certain restrictions in the deed, it was hoped that Dr. Morris would agree to an amendment allowing the desired development if it would benefit the City and enable the Fair tradition to continue.

The portion of the island owned by the City comprised about forty acres, and the terrain was level and above the high water mark, making it ideal for a race track and amusement park or industrial exposition. Developers who examined the property were confident that a good half mile track could be graded at a minimal expense, while leaving ample room for buildings and a driveway around the track for parked cars. The article pointed out that Oneonta was still included in the Central New York Racing Circuit, and if the new park was developed soon enough, the existing racing schedule could be retained. The proposed fair never materialized, but the Webb Island site would be developed in the summer of 1949, when a diligent but unfruitful attempt was made to resurrect the Central New York Fair.

Belmont Park — Yesterday and Today

Top: Two views of the Belmont Park area. Bottom: Concrete retaining wall and piers from the original Grandstand along St. Mary's Lane behind the Fox Nursing Home.

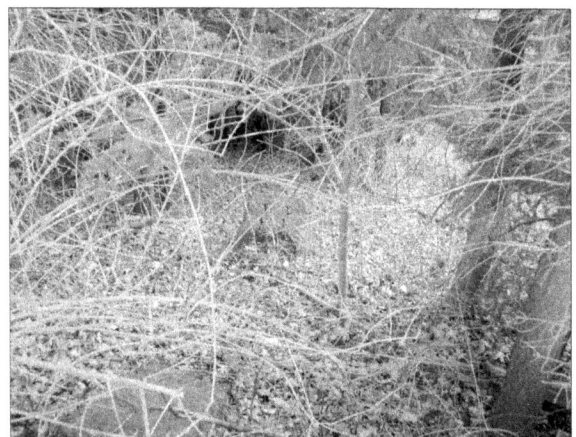

A Brief Encore

In 1949, a determined effort was made to resurrect the Central New York Fair, and the site chosen was Webb Island, the same location suggested by D.F. Keyes in 1927. This new Fair would have some similarities to the original event, but its' structure would be much different. It was to be free to the public, with a fifty-cent charge for Grandstand shows during the day and one dollar at night. The new Fair would have traditional attractions, such as machinery and commercial displays, in addition to Midway rides, side shows, and stage acts. A sight never seen at the old Fair would be Frank Wirtz's Twenty Girl Revue, doing a daily performance of "Swing Out the News."

The new Fair was modeled after the famous "Free Fair" of Iona, Wisconsin. Ross Mannings' Shows provided the Midway attractions which included a musical featuring girls, but Fair Chairman Ernest (Dutch) Damaschke made it clear that the show was not risqué. In June, a half-mile oval track had been graded in preparation for possible horse races. The Fair was scheduled to open on Monday, July 25 at 10:00 a.m., and continue for six days and six nights. Over the weekend, twenty-four tents were erected for machinery and commercial exhibits, and carnival workers were busy setting up rides, while Ray Burgott of Oneonta was fogging the grounds to wipe out the mosquito population. The roadway and track were well watered with sprinklers, and finishing touches were put on the 40 by 60-foot stage for performers.

Opening day of the new Fair was Youth Day, and $150 in prizes would be awarded for a variety of contests. For girls under fourteen, there was a sack race, a balloon race, and a barrel race. For boys under fourteen, there were barrel races, tug-of-war, and a peanut scramble.

Unfortunately, heavy rains made for low attendance on opening day and forced the postponement of the Youth Day contests. While the Managers had been concerned about dust, the grounds instead were covered with mud puddles. The small crowd in the Grandstand enjoyed

Bobby Dae and Babs.

an outstanding talent show provided by Frank Wirth, which included 87 year-old Tom Barrett and 75 year-old Minnie Allen doing clog and tap dancing, in addition to Monty Desoca, a trampoline artist, Frank Carr on a high pole, the Florida Trio, a comedy acrobatic act, and Bobby Dae and Babs, a young dance team. Another attraction at the Fair was the armored limousine used by Adolf Hitler in World War II.

The second day of the new Fair had better weather, but late in the day serious problems developed. Mrs. Raymond Gifford of Maple Street filed a report that her son, Conrad, nineteen, had lost $195 at a roulette wheel. This came as a surprise, since police and a special observer hired by the Fair were on hand to keep an eye on the thirty-plus games to try and hold down losses, which resulted in very few dealers doing any business. According to the police report, young Conrad was allowed to win $40, but was paid with a check. Soon he lost it back, and a lot more that he handed over in cash. The young man appeared at the police station more interested in getting his money back than prosecuting, so no warrant was issued. Chairman Damaschke brought the matter to the attention of Ross Manning, and the game operator was removed from the grounds. In addition to the gambling incident, a girlie show was closed down for too much wiggling and too little clothing. Dutch Damaschke stated that Mr. Manning had taken the initiative in closing down the show. The contract between Manning and the Fair clearly stated that gambling and risqué shows would not be permitted.

As it turned out, the gambling incident was not resolved, as the game operator skipped town without making restitution. This brought about a crackdown by the Oneonta police, who found another illegal gambling establishment on the Midway. At this point, the police informed Ross Manning that all places suspected of gambling would be shut down and the Midway was closely watched by police for the duration of the Fair.

Wednesday was Firemen's Day, with over twenty visiting departments taking part in a 7:30 p.m. parade through the city which terminated at the new Fairgrounds, where prizes were awarded. Oneontans who remembered the Central New York Fair recognized a familiar face, William Wain, whose Uncle Herman was a regular at the old Fair, selling candy and popcorn. Although Herman had passed away, his nephew was carrying on the tradition.

The first and last Webb Island Fair ended on a sour note, with the arrest of Raymond Melville, Master of Ceremonies at the Fair. Melville, of New York City, was reported for exposing himself to three women and several children on Saturday evening, in the vicinity of Fair Street. When police apprehended Melville, he was hiding under the Fair Street bridge (over Oneonta Creek), holding his trousers in his hands. The saga of the Oneonta Fair had thus come full circle—the trolley tracks and the souvenir vendors along Fair Street were gone, but one last adventure was played out on the road to Oneonta's greatest memory.

The Fair was never again repeated, but the track and stables were used occasionally for horse shows, and in the fall of 1950 stock car races were held at Webb Island for one season.

The armored Mercedes-Benz limousine used by Adolf Hitler during World War II was a special attraction at the 1949 Fair.

Memories

Edna Gadsby

I have gone through this subway [*see photos on page 41*] to the Oneonta Fair many times —probably starting in 1913, when I was five or six years old, as my people most always attended the Fair until it was discontinued. The concrete subway structure was the main entrance to the Fairgrounds. It was situated in about the same position as the entrance to today's street, North Belmont Circle, and at the head of Fair Street. The street of North Belmont Circle is part of the original race track. There were no turn-off streets of South Belmont Circle or Hudson Street. The race track went over the top of the subway.

As I remember, the ticket office was located at the very left of the subway and the phone where the people in the photo seemed to be looking and facing. I have forgotten what the admission price to the Fair was. On Fair days, the trolley taking the people to the Fair ran up Main Street, turned right on to Otsego Street, and then left on to Fair Street. The trolley was a special open-sided car, not like the regular ones.

You might enjoy the Roof Garden attraction of Dan Sherman, Mable DeForest, and daughter Tessie's vaudeville act—or even hear Teddy Roosevelt's Governor's campaign speech. You might also get a glimpse of George I. Wilber wearing his little straw hat. On the grounds, Herman the Candyman yearly ground out his salt water taffy. The Keenans brought their ponies for the kids to ride. Schools closed for one day, so that they could take in the Fair. All in all, it was a great Fair! Third Street extended down the hill to Fair Street, with one house built on the side hill. You entered the subway, keeping left to go to the Grandstand—a very well built structure—on the north side

The Keenan Ponies.

of North Belmont Circle—built against the hill houses that lined that side of the street today. Opposite the Grandstand was the Roof Garden. On one end of this was the cupola for the race officials.

Thursday was the biggest day of the Fair Week. It was the day of the Floral Parade —not a Rose Bowl parade, by any means! At night, if you weren't too tired from the day's activities at the Fair, you could go to the Oneonta Theater to see a play produced by the Charles K. Champlin Stock Company that always played Fair Week.

Advertisement from the 1924 Fair program.

Gerald S. Wright

My dad, Gerald S. Wright, grew up on Fifth Street in Oneonta, which was right at the top of the bank connecting the Fairgrounds of the Central New York Fair. He was nineteen years old when the Fair ended in 1926. He told me several stories about the Fair.

Since the Fair was held only one week of the year, the Fairgrounds was a great place for neighborhood kids to play ball, fly kites in the open field, or climb on the Grandstand on the other weeks of the year. Dad was one of them. My dad also did something else on the Fairgrounds during the off season. Cars were just beginning to make their presence in Oneonta in 1904. By 1922, there were enough cars so that the City was concerned with safety and installed two traffic lights on Main Street. Well, two years before that, Dad's father got a Model T Ford, but did not know how to drive it. Dad was about fourteen years old at the time. He had worked at Garlick's Farm near Goodyear Lake, since they were relatives, and learned how to drive farm machinery. With that knowledge, he was able to drive the new car. So he and his dad, who was my grandfather, came to the Fairgrounds and my dad taught my grandfather how to drive the Model T Ford!

The Grandstand and main attractions were just down the hill from Fifth Street. At the top of the hill was a high board fence. During Fair Week, the neighbors got out their stepladders and set them up behind the fence. They put a board plank on the top steps between two ladders and sat on it to watch the activities down below at the Fair. They were able to look over the top of the high fence. During the off season, when the Fair was not being held, railroad employees that lived near the top of the bank took down a section of the fence so that they could walk to work using a short cut across the Fairgrounds. My Grandpa was one of the men who used the short cut to get to work. Eventually, the Fair workers took down a section of the fence, stored it in a safe place, and helped out the railroad workers who walked to work.

Dad used to tell an interesting story about the horse races. There was a man named John Chase in Oneonta. He had a horse that used to pull a coal wagon in the winter when he was selling coal. People used coal to heat their houses. Mr. Chase also trained his horse to race at the Fair. The horse was taught to run faster at the command, "Whoa," which normally means to stop. While the horses were racing around the half mile track, John Chase would holler "Whoa!" His horse would run faster, but the others would become confused and slow down. When the judges realized why Mr. Chase was winning the races, they disqualified him from racing.

During the off season, the ticket booths and the fire ambulance were stored in the empty Floral Hall. During the busy Fair, a horse was always hitched to an ambulance carriage or wagon in readiness to go help people in case of an emergency. Once, when the Fair was not in season, my dad and my uncle found the door to Floral Hall unlatched or open. One got on the vehicle and pushed the foot pedal that rang the bell. The other acted like the horse. The next thing they knew, they were riding down Fair Street hill ringing the bell. Someone notified the cops and a cop called "Brownie" came and told them to get the ambulance back to where it belonged. The cop helped them push the vehicle back up Fair Street hill and back to Floral Hall.

There was a game at the Fair at which a person paid money to use a big mallet to hit a pad and send an object up to a gong. The operator gave my dad or my uncle money to use the mallet to hit the gong. Remember, they were just kids. People who were watching thought that if kid could hit the gong, they could also. The operator cheated people out of money. After my dad or my uncle hit the gong, the operator flipped a switch, which made it impossible for the object to strike the gong when adults tried the game. He would then give my dad another chance and flip the switch, so that he seemed to have great strength and hit the gong. More people paid money to try, but could not do it.

As a boy, Dad did not always have the admission money to get into the Fair. He would hang around the admission gate. Once, when he was lingering around outside the main gate, a man came in his buggy and said, "Hop in boy, I'll need your help." Once inside the Fairgrounds, the man said, "Hop off, I don't need your help after all." The man turned out to be George I. Wilber, who organized the Fair. He was kind to the neighborhood kids. At other times, the ticket seller, who was a local neighbor, helped Dad and others get into the Fair by giving them used ticket stubs.

Dad remembered that elm trees grew at the eastern end of the Fair, where North Belmont Circle is today. People used to tie their horses to the trees to be in the shade, while they had fun at the Fair. Apparently, there were three animal barns at the eastern end of what is now South Belmont Circle. They housed cows and sheep. In the early morning, neighborhood people bought milk at the cattle barn for ten cents per gallon. They brought their own containers. Farm machinery was also displayed in that area.

[*The memory above was submitted by Marilyn E. Bailey, the daughter of Gerald S. Wright. She is too young to have memories of the Fair itself, but she added the anecdote on the next page about one of the Fair's colorful characters. – Author*]

When I was a young girl visiting my grandmother at 13 Valleyview Street, there was an older man next door at 11 Valleyview Street who used to give me Black Jack gum over the fence. I remember it came in a blue wrapper and tasted like licorice. The man's name was Floyd Wallace. When I knew him, he was retired from the telephone company and his wife was retired from teaching elementary school in Oneonta. When Floyd Wallace was fifteen years old, he had quite an adventure at the Fair in a helium balloon. Grandma told my brother and me not to mention the balloon adventure to him. He did not like to talk about it.

Esther Bresee

We lived on Otsego Street—at that time considered to be "way out in the country" by my family's friends. It was a pretty pink street (brick) lined with many maples and elms now gone. All the houses had porches on which all one's friends came and sat to review the Floral Parade which always came down that street. It was probably chosen because it was paved and ran into Fair Street, then only one block from the Fairgrounds. Tilton Avenue had trolley tracks and was closer to the grounds. Over these ran an open-air trolley, which was fascinating. I always was sorry we lived so near, I didn't have a chance to ride to the Fair on it.

Otsego & Herkimer open car #94.

In second grade, I was chosen to be a Red Cross nurse on a float. I felt quite thrilled and also very dignified and when it passed my home; my family and their friends waved frantically, I refused to wave back—to their great disappointment. Somehow as a Red Cross nurse, it seemed beneath my dignity to be so childish. But now, did you ever see a parade where no one waved? Even Miss America and the political figures all wave!

On all streets leading to the Fair, people set up stands to sell baked goods, popcorn balls, candy fans, hot dogs and all kinds of gimmicks. Living so near the grounds, many people rented rooms to the Fair people and visitors. My father allowed my mother to do this during Fair Week. One time, I was very impressed as we had "The Girl in the Golden Globe." Constructed on the Roof Garden, facing the Grandstand, it was metal mesh in a bronze-gold color. She was a blonde and wore a gold suit and helmet, and rode a motorcycle round and round and up and over inside the globe. It seemed very glamorous.

When it came time to leave, her husband tried to pay the room rent, which was no more than two or three dollars, with a hundred dollar bill. Naturally, we didn't have change on hand for that amount, to say nothing of ever having seen a bill of that size anywhere. My father demanded exact payment and they did have it. We always wondered if the big bill was good or if they were trying to pull a "fast one" on us. Fair Week , always the week after the State Fair, brought Roof Garden acts; horses, racing, and trotting; it was usually about the second or third week of September and it was usually hot and dusty. No air conditioning—hand held fans were the order of the day and many carried advertising. There were flies too—hordes of them, attracted by the animals, and the fruit and food tents. Another thing to beware of, besides flies, were pickpockets when the Midway was wall-to-wall people.

The Midway, now Hudson Street, was always fun for old and young—specially the latter with a bit of pocket money to spend. The booths were filled with enticing objects and goodies and games to play. I was interested by a celluloid desk set, which I still have. There was always a Ferris wheel and a merry-go-round. The handiwork, food, and vegetable tents always offered ribbons—the prizes and competition were good and looked forward to.

Naturally, Fair Street got its name because it led directly into the Fairgrounds. It become a street in 1873. Belmont Circle, as you now know it, and as you would expect, was the race track. The left bank was a natural for the Grandstand. The Fair, along with traveling circuses, the Chautauqua, and the repertory, an opera company, brought amusement and culture to the small cities of the land. They were a great part of our early Americana and offered much to our more quiet ways of life in those days.

Special events have always brought together great numbers of people. Special events like hot air balloon ascensions, air-stunting by the biplanes, the majestic dirigibles, Herman Candy, popcorn balls, trapeze artists, horse races, and Grandstand events kept people from being bored between races. In town, the Charles K. Champlain Repertory Company almost always played the Oneonta Theater that week. The theater was half the size it is now, but still had two balconies.

Ad page from the 1924 Fair program.

A Central New York Fair Postcard Album

Bringing the Stock to the Fair.   ONEONTA FAIR

LARGE CROWD AT ONEONTA FAIR

Central New York Fair, Oneonta, N. Y., 1909.

Central New York Fair, Oneonta, N. Y., 1909

Central New York Fair, Oneonta, N. Y.

Central New York Fair, Oneonta, N. Y.,

110—"Billy Williams" at Oneonta, (N. Y.) Fair, 1908.

Central New York Fair, Oneonta, N. Y. 1899

Central New York Fair, Oneonta, N. Y.,

Central New York Fair, Oneonta, N. Y., 1909

Central New York Fair, Oneonta, N. Y.

Central New York Fair, Oneonta, N. Y.,

H.W.SHELDON
HORSEMARKET.

THE PINES
HOLSTEIN FRIESIAN CATTLE

Central New York Fair, Oneonta, N. Y., 1909

Central New York Fair, Oneonta, N. Y.,

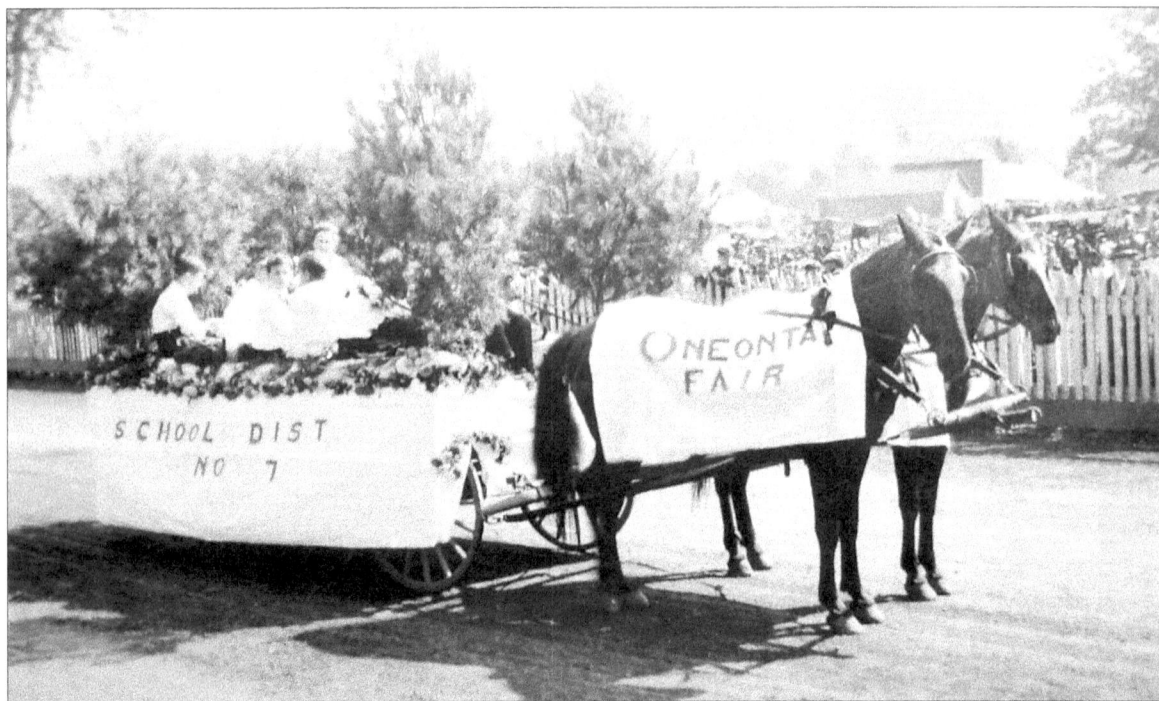

INDEX

www.ingramcontent.com/pod-product-compliance
Lightning Source LLC
Chambersburg PA
CBHW050355100426
42739CB00015BB/3399